W9-BKF-202

WINNING
IN THE
5th QUARTER

Apply the Secrets
of Football to Your
Life-Strategy Playbook

BOB BECK

MORGAN JAMES PUBLISHING • NEW YORK

WINNING
IN THE
5th QUARTER

Copyright © 2008 Bob Beck

No part of this publication may be reproduced or transmitted in any form or by any means, mechanical or electronic, including photocopying and recording, or by any information storage and retrieval system, without permission in writing from author or publisher (except by a reviewer, who may quote brief passages and/or show brief video clips in review).

ISBN: 978-1-60037-455-5 (Paperback)
ISBN: 978-1-60037-456-2 (Hardback)
Library of Congress Control Number: 2008928169

Published by:

MORGAN · JAMES
THE ENTREPRENEURIAL PUBLISHER ™
www.morganjamespublishing.com

Morgan James Publishing, LLC
1225 Franklin Ave Ste 32
Garden City, NY 11530-1693
Toll Free 800-485-4943
www.MorganJamesPublishing.com

Cover/Interior Design by:
Rachel Lopez
rachel@r2cdesign.com

Habitat for Humanity®
Peninsula
Building Partner

Dedication

TO MY SON ROBBIE *who has brought me more pride, love, and great memories than I could possibly express in words. You inspire more people, in more ways, than you know.*

To my wife, Laurie, for her love, support, and encouragement which make all things possible. You could possibly be the most courageous and inspirational person I know.

Acknowledgments

COACH KEN HATFIELD, for being such a fantastic role model and leader for my son to emulate and all the young men that had the privilege to play for him.

Coach Larry Brinson, for also being such a committed caretaker of the young men he coaches. Also special thanks for his belief in my son and recruiting him with such passion and dignity.

Coach Allan Chadwick, who sets the foundation for success and sets the standard for every young man who is fortunate to play in his program.

David Hancock, founder Morgan James Publishing, for his belief and support in publishing this book.

Gerhard Gschwandner, publisher and founder of *Selling Power Magazine* for his support, encouragement, and for sharing his network with me.

Dr Patricia Ross of Mile High Editing whose editing helped make my all words make sense.

Susan Karnovsky, for her input into the edits that were made on this book. They made a tremendous difference to what you are about to read.

Chuck Carey, who is always so supportive and has such passion. He helped me with this book in many ways.

Betsey Cagle, who was brave enough to read and help me edit the very first, extremely rough draft.

Of course I have to acknowledge my wife, Laurie, who is my reason for everything I do; Melissa, Tyler, and Nick who inspire me in ways they don't even know about; and, of course, Robbie, for all the great moments and the love and trust he gives to me.

Testimonials

"*Winning in the 5th Quarter* is a thesis on success, life, love and joy. This book will be a must read for anyone wanting to enjoy life to its fullest."

COACH KEN HATFIELD

Coach Hatfield was one of the most successful college football coaches in history. He led highly successful college football programs at Air Force, Clemson, and Rice University. He also coached at Tennessee and Florida.

"This book captures what every player and parent needs to understand about the game of football! I will make sure my players and my own kids read this book."

COACH LARRY BRINSON

Coach Brinson played five years in the National Football League, including three seasons with the Dallas Cowboys and two years with the Seattle Seahawks. Brinson was a member of the Dallas teams that played in the 1978 and 1979 Superbowls. Brinson has been a college football coach for 24 years. Currently he is a successful football coach for the University of Kentucky.

"This book is nothing less than a guide for lifelong success. The messages and concepts are timeless. They will have a profound impact on everyone that reads this book and more importantly uses it to create a foundation for happiness and achievement."

GRANT TEAFF

Executive Director of American Football Coaches Association. One of the most effective administrators in intercollegiate athletics, in 2002, the Sporting News ranked Teaff as one of the most powerful administrators of college athletics. In December 2004, Teaff was named one of the most influential people in college sports by Street & Smith's Sports Business Journal. Teaff's outstanding career as a college coach has placed him in eight Halls of Fame.

"As someone who has not grown up in the US, I had not seen a football game until I was 29. Once I understood the game, I was hooked. Later I had the privilege to meet people like Fran Tarkenton, Roger Staubach and Terry Bradshaw who applied the rules of the game to a second career that led them to far greater success. Bob Beck has extracted the success DNA from the game of football and cloned it so it can grow into a winning game plan in the reader's conscious mind. It's a book worth sharing with people who want to transform, grow and enjoy their life to the fullest."

GERHARD GSCHWANDTNER

Founder and Publisher SELLING POWER Winner of 3 Gold Awards American Society of Business Publication Editors

"Thank you for writing this book. Now I can finally relate to my son like my husband does."

EBONY ANDERSON

Author of the book "If I was just a Little Taller"

"Winning in the 5th Quarter is timeless classic. I discovered new ways to appreciate the game of football. Whether you are a fan or not people should read this book. Everyone should really enjoy and learn a lot about how to succeed and be happy in their lives by adopting the principles of the 5th quarter."   LORETTA LAROCHE

She has had six television specials air on 80 PBS stations across the country. She has been nominated for local and prime time Emmy Awards, has appeared on CNN, ABC and NBC affiliates. She has authored 7 books, Is on the council for the Mass General Center for Anxiety and Depression. She was recently awarded the National Humor Treasure Award.

"Finally someone as put down on paper what football is all about. I couldn't put it down. These words have needed to be written for years. I am glad Bob Beck finally put it all together!"   CHIP SMITH

Founder and President of Competitive Edge Sports.

Chip is recognized as one of the foremost speed and strength experts in the United States. Chip has trained over 200 current NFL players and does combine preparation for scores of players selected each year in the NFL Draft.

"We tell players that attend Rice University they are attending for fifty years not just four. We talk to them about the 5ᵗʰ Quarter their first day here. Bob Beck has expressed this message in the exact way I would like every player and parent to understand. This book will become part of our culture."   COACH DAVID BAILIFF

Coach Bailiff is head football coach of Rice University. He has been preparing young men for the 5ᵗʰ quarter for years. He has successfully coached at Texas Christian University and Texas State University before heading up the Rice football program.

Table of Contents

Foreword

A LOT OF PEOPLE DON'T "get" football. For people who don't watch the game and don't really understand it, they think football is just a bunch of guys beating up on each other as each team tries to get a ball across the other team's goal line. And, what's worse, some people tend to believe the stereotype that football players are not too smart, playing this seemingly simple-minded game.

For many who play the game, or for parents who have talented youngsters who love to play, they often tend to stress statistics—the number of yards per carry, the number of tackles or receptions. While these are all the indicators that tell you how well you played an individual game, they don't really tell you what football is all about.

If you play football or are an avid fan, you all think that the most important quarter of the game is the fourth quarter. Sure, that's when many individual games are won or lost, but ultimately that's not the most important quarter in football. Bob Beck's book, *Winning in the 5th Quarter*, finally divulges the secret that many of us players know but no one has ever been able to successfully get down on paper. In fact, I wanted to write this forward because *finally*, someone "gets" what's important about the game of football.

Let's face it; a football game is just a game. It's fun to win them; it's definitely fun to win championships, and we all know how heartbreaking it is when our team loses. But, as Beck says in the introduction: "Football isn't just about spending sixty minutes on a rectangular, chalk-lined field of green and walking away either a winner or a loser." It's the lessons that you take from the football field into life that count. It's the lessons of commitment and hard work, of handling loss, and of having the courage to make hard decisions both on the field and off.

For those of us who play or have played the game, Beck stresses one of the most widely known but little talked about facts of the game. Regardless what level of play or how far you go in football, unless you become a coach, it ends at an early age. But, what do you do with the rest of your life? All the attention you get as a player, as well as the rush of winning, is addictive. But, if you stop playing at eighteen, twenty-two, or even forty-two, you have your whole life ahead of you. Again, *what do you do*? You listen to Bob Beck when he says that it's the lessons you take from football into the *fifth* quarter, the game of life, that tells you how really successful you were in football.

Beck stresses that football is a microcosm of life, and I absolutely agree with him that learning the secret of football will help you to achieve true success in any aspect of your life. And what I like best about the guy is that he's lived his words. He played sports when he was younger, and from the lessons he learned, he's started multiple businesses and turned them into very successful ventures. But most important, because of football, he raised his son—the star of this book—with the right values and the right attitude about the game itself. The father made sure that the son knew that what he learned on the field could be taken off the field and into life.

Winning in the 5ᵗʰ Quarter leverages the lessons of football—for everyone. I definitely want my kids to read this book. I urge all parents who have kids who play football—or any sport for that matter—to read this book. And even if you just are a football fan or someone who needs a boost in life, you'll find inspiration to move forward in these pages.

Let's all take a page out of this playbook!

To your success!

P. _____.

(Due to contractual reasons, the author of this forward is unable to divulge their full name.)

Introduction

The Secret of Football

Lessons for Success in Life

I'VE WRITTEN THIS BOOK BECAUSE I want to share what I've learned about life from my favorite game, football. This may or may not be your favorite game, but this sport has given so much to me. Whatever your feelings about it, whether or not you've ever had any involvement with football on any level, I'm glad you have this book in your hands now.

No matter who you are or where you are in life, the secret of football is for you, too. I am totally convinced that once you learn the secret of the game, you'll be able to succeed in whatever you choose to do.

The attributes and principles of success that are detailed in this book will change and enhance every aspect of your life. Whether you've ever suited up and taken the field or even if you've never seen a football game, the core values, acceptance and execution of the principles discussed in this book will make a difference in your personal success and fulfillment in your life.

Football isn't just about spending sixty minutes on a rectangular, chalk-lined field of green and walking away either a winner or a loser. It's about how practice, discipline, victories, losses, hard work, team play, focus, competitive spirit, and creativity transcend the contests that are played each fall weekend. The game is a microcosm of life. Learning the secret of football can and will contribute enormously to achieving true success in any aspect of your life.

Most football teams stress the fourth quarter as the most important part of the game to their players. They say that the fourth quarter is when the game is won or lost; when you and your team succeed or fail. But really, the *only* quarter that matters at all is the one everyone plays after their playing days are done. I call it your *fifth* quarter.

The fifth quarter is the ongoing game we all play, the game of life. It's 24/7, 365 days long, and it doesn't stop when the referee blows a whistle. It's *your* game. How you handle the opportunities that come your way will determine whether you win or lose.

I want you to win. And once you understand and use football's secret, your fifth quarter will be one of triumph.

Students from six to sixty, college grads about to embark on a new career, fledgling entrepreneurs, established executives, CEOs, retirees—you're all in the game. There are no benchwarmers in the fifth quarter! And the fifth quarter has all the elements of football—there is a playing field, other players, rules to follow, obstacles to overcome, goals to go for, and wins and losses along the way. If you know and use the secret of football, every moment in your fifth quarter can result in the sweet fruits of success and victory.

I've done my best to apply this secret in my life. Without exaggerating,

I can say that I am winning. I am not and never have been a professional, college, or even a high school football coach. However, I have played just about every sport out there at one point or another, including water polo, bocce ball, swimming, diving, bowling, running, wrestling, golf, basketball, hockey, baseball, diving, skiing, tennis, and I've even ridden a horse or two. I also played college football and I am the proud father of a football player—he's one of the many successful people you'll meet in this book.

I've also taken three companies public, turned around a failing company, am a board member for a publicly held company, written and published other books, and I currently own my own successful speaking, sales training and consulting company. I am married to the women of my dreams, and we are blessed with four outstanding children.

When people ask me how I am able to do all that I've done in my life, I tell them the truth: every single one of my accomplishments comes from understanding and applying the secret of football.

I want to share this secret with you. I want to help you use it in your life. As such, I've included many exercises and drills for you throughout the book. I hope you enjoy doing them. They are here to help you win.

I sincerely hope that the secret of football helps you achieve every goal you set for yourself in your life's fifth quarter.

CHAPTER ONE

THE COIN TOSS

CHOICES AND CHANGE

When you're finished changing, you're finished.
BENJAMIN FRANKLIN

I f the coach hadn't quit my son's peewee football team, I may not be writing this book. The day I was asked to step in and take over, I made a choice that was a major turning point for both me and my son Robbie. Did I know it then? Nope. But, as they say, hindsight is always twenty-twenty. I look back to that moment as the true beginning of this book.

Robbie made up his mind that he wanted to be a football player when he was just six years old—not that my obvious love of the game had anything to do with it, of course. He signed up for a peewee team in the flag football league. For those of you who are unfamiliar with flag football, it's basically "football lite"—a much kinder, gentler game in which grabbing a handkerchief velcro'd to the ball carrier's belt substitutes for tackling. It provides a nice introduction to the sport for little kids, with minimal chance of injuries.

My son's peewee team was a total disaster. Watching from the stands, I could plainly see that Robbie's coach lacked any understanding whatsoever of football strategy. Not surprisingly, Robbie's team was losing every game. To me, winning is not the be-all and end-all. However, when kids realize that they're losing because they don't know how to play properly, they can get very discouraged.

When I was named to replace the coach who quit, it would have been easy to say no. I was a busy executive. I wasn't a professional athlete, and I certainly wasn't a brilliant football strategist. But I knew one thing for sure: I could help those kids understand that success or failure was a choice that they could make.

That's the very first principle of the secret of football and the secret of life: success is a choice

You can choose success. Anyone can. And once you understand and tune in to the inner game, football prepares you for choosing success. This is true whether you are a coach, player, parent of a player, dedicated fan, Sunday afternoon couch potato, or someone who has never watched a game in his or her life.

Making the right choices begins early. In fact, the process starts before you're really able to make informed choices at all. Since I'd been at the earlier games (all losses), I knew what I was inheriting: a group of kids who were in no sense of the word a team. Change was an absolute necessity. As with the rest of life, I knew that *if something isn't working, you change it.* Arnold Schwarzenegger may say, "No pain, no gain." I prefer to say, "No *change*, no gain."

There is a second principal of success that is closely related to the first: in order to achieve change, you have to make changes. This may seem too painfully obvious or even redundant, but it isn't. Many people who want to *change* their fortunes are unwilling to *make the changes necessary* to bring that about. Some lack the necessary courage. Others simply don't know how.

Part of the problem with Robbie's flag football team was that he and many of his teammates were playing out of position. That is so basic. The first thing you do with a prospective player is find out what he's good at and play him where he can use his talents. Distributing players randomly across the field without regards to each one's specific abilities will bring you certain failure.

The kids on that team were yearning to be more successful, and I wanted to help them get there. I knew what to do, and I knew how to do it. I also understood that success wasn't going to happen without wholesale changes. So I made them.

First, I switched Robbie from offensive lineman to receiver. He was the fastest player on the team. I knew from tossing the football in our backyard that he had good hands, too. It made absolutely no sense that these attributes hadn't been utilized. It's not that blockers aren't as important as receivers. They are. But we had bigger kids who could do just as good a job or better at those positions.

Next, I designed a simple pass play and added it to the team's very skimpy playbook. Like all the other coaches in this league, the former coach hadn't designed any pass plays. He lacked the confidence that players this young could pull off a pass — this despite the fact that we had a quarterback who threw pretty well.

I believed in my kids. I drilled them on this new wrinkle. And in my first game as coach, I put my money where my mouth was: I tried a pass on the first play from scrimmage. It was a quick toss to Robbie. The other team was lined up, as usual, to defend against a run. I thought a pass play would catch them by surprise. It did.

Our quarterback dropped back and Robbie broke free over the middle. The pass was right on the money. Robbie cradled the ball and took off at full speed. No one had a chance to catch him. Seventy yards later, he crossed the goal line, scoring the first touchdown of his life.

This one play turned the team around and put it on the road to a rewarding season. Robbie was deservedly all smiles.

This story has two points.

1. Life is about making choices, and that usually means making changes.

2. Once you choose to succeed, you must also choose *where* to succeed.

All of the hard work and dedication you put into your sport or your career won't add up to much if you're playing the wrong position. If you weigh a hundred and eighty pounds, you're not going to make it as a defensive tackle; if you weigh two-eighty, forget about trying out for tailback.

In order to realize your goals, you must put yourself in the right situation. You must make choices that allow you to utilize your abilities to the max.

Otherwise, you are going to underachieve. Even worse, you might give up on yourself.

So, I want you to ask yourself two questions right now: *am I doing what I should be doing?* If the answer is *no,* acknowledge that. Then ask yourself: *What's stopping me from reaching my full potential?* Am I working with the wrong coach, taking bad advice? Am I on the wrong team? Or is it that I haven't yet found what I want to commit myself to with a single-minded purpose? Have I avoided chasing my dream, either out of a perceived lack of opportunity or a fear of failure?

If you answered yes to any of these questions, ask yourself: what can I do to change? This is another way of saying: *how well can I prepare myself to succeed in life, doing what I want to do?* Once you make that decision and act on it, you'll ignite your self-esteem—a powerful element indeed!

Nothing fuels self-esteem more than success. Success on the football field is never wholly determined by points on the scoreboard. Even if your team loses, you can still walk off the field a winner. Losing is tough. But you can bolster your confidence immeasurably by knowing you played at your highest level.

For Robbie, that first touchdown transformed him. At that moment, even though he was only six years old, he knew he was a competitor, a *player.* He knew that all the work he'd put into practice was worth it. It was a feeling he would always retain.

That touchdown changed his teammates, too. More so than any other sport, football depends on teamwork. After that first successful pass play, his teammates knew they could compete. They believed they were capable of scoring and winning. And they did.

That day, Robbie decided to succeed in life. In my mind Robbie's success in life all traces back to that one play. Does a single childhood accomplishment make a life? No. Could we have predicted his future, back when he was only six? Of course not. From that day forward, Robbie faced the same challenges we all face in growing up. But the success of that moment instilled in him, at a very early age, the conviction that he *could* succeed. And it all started with that one play that enabled Robbie and his teammates to change their viewpoint about themselves: they now saw themselves as winners!

INCH BY INCH

Football is a game of inches. Many games are won or lost every week by just a few inches. The game of life is the same way. Regardless of Robbie's achievements on the football field, he didn't immediately go on to become the star, the team leader, the BMOC (Big Man on Campus) or a corporate executive. Neither will you. However, as long as you are moving forward at a reasonable pace, you are making progress. The trick is to keep moving forward and to extend your reach.

In football, you have four attempts to move the ball ten yards. If the team can't accomplish this, they have to punt the ball to the other team. Then they try something different the next time they get the ball. In the same way, you should give yourself a reasonable amount of time to move your ball down the field of life. If you don't make it in the time frame you allotted for yourself, you might need to punt and try something different.

When I consult with companies and individuals who are not moving at the pace they want, I always challenge them with this concept of being able to change. To me, it is a natural thought process to clearly see that if actions are not netting you the desired result, then change is easy. However, change is against human nature. On the other hand, doing the same thing over and over and expecting a different result makes no sense either. It takes work, commitment, sacrifice and dedication in order to change.

You've got to push yourself forward. When you get there, continue to push. You will be surprised just how far you can go with this approach. Too often in today's society, people think someone owes them something just because they exist. There is an underlying feeling from a lot of younger people I work with in various organizations that just showing up everyday is good enough; that following the crowd will take them to the top of the mountain. This is very far from the truth. This viewpoint will retard anyone's growth.

I often wonder where this thinking comes from. I have never run into this mode of thinking from any ex-football player. With further investigation of this perplexing mindset, you'll find that we often seek to protect and shield the people around us. We try to make sure they don't feel the pain or frustration of making mistakes or of failing. We might sound the referee's whistle of caution at every turn: "Don't bite off more than you can chew," or "Stop and smell the roses," or "Be happy with what you have." But, "When is enough, enough"?

These lowered expectations can be a real disservice to people. We all need to push ourselves. We all need coaches who teach us to reach for the stars. We may not come away with any, but we will come away with a lot more than if we had not tried. All success has a price, whether you're in the game of football or the game of life. Without some pain, sacrifice, stress, and tension there is no growth. No pain, no change, no gain. We all have to risk the short-term, uncomfortable feelings connected with exploring the new avenues that will offer us long-term gain and ultimate success.

So remember the basic principals in this first chapter: success is a choice. Put yourself in a situation that allows you to maximize your abilities, and if you haven't done that, then change your situation.

CHAPTER TWO

PRE-GAME HUDDLE
COMMITMENT

The quality of a man's life is in direct proportion to his commitment to
excellence, regardless of his chosen field of endeavor.
COACH VINCE LOMBARDI

When you decide you want to achieve anything, the real work begins. It requires pure dedication and true commitment. That's the next secret to success and what this chapter is all about.

Webster's defines "commitment" as the state or an instance of being obligated or emotionally impelled.[1] Everyone would certainly agree you have to have a commitment to play any sport. The essence of the word "commit" is from Latin roots and means cutting away from. When you are committed to something or someone, you are cutting out all your other options and other possibilities. You are also cutting away all the justifications and excuses for not following through. Unfortunately, not everyone understands what commitment means or how to apply the meaning of the word. It's not a natural phenomenon. It's an acquired, hard-earned trait.

Football players understand this or they don't make it. They learn all kinds of lessons that don't come naturally to any of us. Getting up at the break of dawn to run a few miles; running full speed into someone who is twice your size; laying out to catch a ball; spending endless hours watching films; and lifting weights until you can't move your arms are just a few of the "unnatural" routines a player commits to. Which one of these would be considered natural acts for you? I would guess none.

All sports include "unnatural" elements. The continuous practice and reinforcement of these unnatural elements is one of the ways football differs from any other sport and makes it the greatest game on earth. What really separates the men from the boys is the reinforcement that football necessitates.

For example, if everyday life was like football, every time you made a mistake, someone would blindside you, knocking you into next week. How would that motivate you to learn? I would guess you wouldn't make that same

---

1   Webster's Ninth New Collegiate Dictionary, s.v. "commitment."

mistake twice. The point is, if a football player does not execute what he has learned and practice it everyday there is a negative consequence waiting for him around every corner. That is exactly how it works in the world outside of sports too, whether you realize it or not.

A lot of what one must do to play football does not come naturally. Football is a tough game, but life outside of sports is an even a tougher game. In life, we don't have the cheering crowds offering us the positive reinforcement players get when they execute well. We don't have hordes of coaches consistently teaching, encouraging and correcting everything we do. Most of us certainly don't have a group of teammates blocking for us, knocking down obstacles as we make our way to the goal line of success. Ultimately, everyone finds out that you have to count on yourself. If you want to achieve any level of success in your life it's up to you. In football, players learn early and often what it takes to be successful. It is reinforced at every practice, every game, and even in the off-season. The trick is to convert lessons learned on the field to the game of life.

All players hang up their cleats at some point. For some of them, the attributes of success they learned on the field become part of their core being. These are the players who truly understand the secret of football. For some reason, other former players struggle to translate the lessons learned in football. They have been unable to make them their foundation in life.

It doesn't matter if you were a benchwarmer and hardly saw time in a game or if you were an All-Pro NFL player, the lessons and teachings are the same. The time and level of reinforcement of those lessons or the thickness of the foundation might be a little different, but the principle attributes of success learned remain the same. It is at the core of the game of football. Certainly if you played four years in college or made it to the professional level, you not only have a solid foundation built, you have a beautiful framed-in dream house in the works!

A football player's work ethic, practice, discipline and learning all should transfer easily to the game of life. If a player does not implement these learned skills in the game of life, they can forget them and struggle unnecessarily. The good news is, when a player truly learns something and practices it for any period of time, it will come back once he rededicates himself to the discipline needed to regain that skill. If you haven't ridden a bike in a while, you could still get on one and peddle down the street. You might wobble a little at first, or you may wreck because you have temporarily lost your skill of zooming down the street peddling with no hands, but if you persist, the skills will come back.

If you have never played football nor any other sport for that matter, does that mean you are doomed to failure or mediocrity? Of course not! You'll be glad to know there is still hope for you. Seriously, you can learn the principle attributes of success in other ways. The fact that you are reading this book is a great first step. But just like football, you will have to practice things that may not come naturally to you. You'll have to employ a disciplined routine that you follow daily. You will also have to measure your progress and implement any needed adjustments. Football players just get a chance to set their foundations earlier in life. They have a reinforcement process that is next to none. If they are on a team, they have no choice but to put into practice what they have learned. As early as six years old, they get to start laying in the foundations that they can then build upon throughout their lives.

If you have never played a sport or were not fortunate enough to participate in the game of football, you have to establish the same kind of foundation in order to reach your full potential in life. As you read the succeeding chapters you will be able to relate them to your everyday life and begin laying your foundation.

INSIDE DEDICATION

Recently, I was watching the HBO program called *Inside the NFL*. It is a program that shows the highlights of the previous week's professional games, reviews the games that are scheduled for the following week, and discusses current topics around the NFL. Successful professionals who know the game, many of whom are ex-players and coaches, host the show. In this particular segment they were talking about commitment. They described how NFL players had to take their roles more seriously by showing more of a commitment in the off-season. They talked about off-season weight programs, running, and staying in better shape.

Wow, that was stunning to me. NFL players get paid high six or seven figure incomes. They make a living with their bodies and yet they have to be called out to show more commitment? Amazing! Every high school player understands that they have to have at least that level of commitment if they want to even make the team, let alone excel. So not even all of the most successful athletes understand how vital real commitment is to success.

Think about this as it relates to your own life:

- Just because you go to class does not mean you are a student.

- Just because you can sing a song does not necessarily mean you're a singer. (My wife will attest to this one for sure.)

- Just because you sell something does not necessarily mean you're a salesperson.

- Just because you're in a profession does not mean you're a professional.

- Just because you are on the team doesn't mean you're a player.

Successful students, singers, salespeople, football players and other professionals have developed the skill of being totally committed physically, mentally, and emotionally. The only way you'll ever get the most out of anything is if you totally commit to doing it!

IQ

The game of football demands a much different level of commitment than most other sports. As I said, football players make a living with their bodies. They don't have a horse to ride, a car to drive, or a boat to race. It is their physical and mental abilities that determine their success. Some players have to be committed to put on weight; others have to be committed to lose it. All players need to strive to be faster and stronger. There is a strong correlation between the level of commitment a player has in off-season conditioning programs to the possible injuries during the season. If an athlete is injured, it is very hard to excel, make a contribution, or even play.

The physical commitment is not the only commitment needed to succeed in football. There are some misconceived notions that football players are dumb or not as intelligent as people in other sports. I have to laugh at this notion. Anyone who thinks this way should just pick up a fifth-grade playbook sometime and see if they can understand it.

At one point in my life I thought I would make a good football coach. Was I in for a shock! Though I played the game at the college level, I quickly found out that there was much I didn't know. I read through my son's fifth-grade team playbook. It had so many different formations, plays, schemes and defensive plays, I could barely understand it. Football takes a lot of thought and a high level of intelligence.

The commitment goes far beyond the weight room, track, or football field. It's an ongoing learning process. Players spend hours watching films of themselves and their opponents. They try to pick up the smallest traits to get an advantage. There are always new formations and plays being created by every team and by their opponents. Show me a coach or a player who feels they have it all figured out and I'll show you a player or coach who the game has passed by.

Consider the commitment it takes, both mentally and physically, to play the game of football. Let's compare it to the sport of boxing, as just one example. Sure, boxing is physically demanding and there is also a strategy involved, but I know for a fact that boxing strategy isn't nearly as complicated as a football playbook. Now, to be fair, the best boxers, like football players, watch films to discover the tendencies of their opponents. There is no question you have to be committed to be a boxer. It is different than football, though. Boxers are evenly matched by weight, they have padded gloves, and there is only one other person opposing them. In football, just imagine you are a running back or a quarterback. You have eleven guys trying to knock you out, not just one. It is not uncommon to have more than a one-hundred-pound weight differential between players and there are times when more than one person may actually be trying to hurt you on purpose!

PRIORITIES

What usually comes with commitment is the ability to decide what your priorities are and stick to your decision to keep those priorities at the top of the page. Many times this means you have to give up something wonderful to keep that priority at the top of the page. This can come in the form of time, effort, money, or even physical effort. The people who understand the secret of football are very aware of this fact because commitment to your priorities is one of the secrets of life as well. Reflect on the people you might be familiar with who are successful. To keep the balance between their families, friends, and careers, wouldn't you agree that they've very likely had to make huge commitments and choices? Now think about those who have less commitment or who struggle with figuring out what's really important.

Not everyone who has reached the pinnacle of their sport understands this as deeply as they need to. You can't be committed once in awhile, that's like being a little bit married or a little bit pregnant; either you are married or you're not. Either you're pregnant or you're not. You are either committed or you're not. There's no middle ground when it comes to commitment.

Take the case of William Perry, better known as the "Fridge." Can you believe he ate himself out of a job and a career? The Chicago Bears had a weight restriction for Perry. At first, when he would exceed these restrictions they fined him thousands of dollars. I think they required he weigh somewhere less than four hundred pounds. The "Fridge" had to decide what was important and then commit to losing weight. Give me a break. I think Perry is only six-foot two-inches, so four hundred pounds would be hard for most of us to even reach, let alone exceed. Please, someone call me and offer me millions of dollars along with fame and fortune for keeping my weight under a figure that should be easily attainable.

The "Fridge" continued to eat. He got slower and fatter and was eventually released by the Bears. When was the last time you heard anything about William Perry, a man who was once a household name? The last time I saw the "Fridge" he was boxing Manute Bol in a celebrity-boxing match. I think the word "celebrity" was loosely used in this case. Who knows how far the "Fridge" could have gone if he'd decided to commit to keeping his weight at a reasonable level?

The best story I remember about commitment comes out of the book *Think and Grow Rich* by Napoleon Hill. From this ageless book of wisdom comes the story "Burning the Ships." Supposedly, there was a battle fought in the 1600's. There was a wooden ship full of warriors ready to storm an island where the battle was to be fought. As soon as the last warrior was off the ship and they were all poised on the beach ready to start the battle the commander's first order was to *burn the ships! Burn the ships!* What kind of order was that? Had he lost his mind? On the surface it certainly appeared that way. Think about it though, if they burned the ships, the only way to survive on the island was to win the battle. Talk about commitment!

In the game of football, you have to make a commitment right from the beginning. It really doesn't matter at what level you play. In most cities kids strap on the pads at about eight years old. Even at eight, the kids learn quickly who is committed. The ones who are less committed are likely to get their blocks knocked off. If they are tentative on the field or not committed to their assignments, when they go to make a block or tackle, they will soon be picking themselves up off the field and wondering what happened. After that occurs a few times even the slowest learners figure it out.

That's why it was so surprising to me to hear these ex-professional super-stars talk about the professional players' level of commitment in the NFL. You would think by now they would have figured it out.

The Fridge's story is an extreme example of consequences that stems from a lack of commitment. There are many ways to measure commitment. If we refer back to the original definition we find it's an instance of being obligated or emotionally impelled. Using that definition, we can focus on specific areas. One way to measure commitment is to have the discipline to set goals and do what it takes to achieve them. Making it up as you go along is not a winning strategy in sports, business, or life. You have to set a course and follow your dream. Success doesn't happen by accident. You have to commit to success and execute against the list of goals you have put in front of yourself. In other words, you have to have a committed plan full of actions and results.

Do you realize how much planning goes into each football game? Once you hit the high school level the sacrifices by both players and coaches is admirable. The players have to all but learn a new language; they have to commit to two-a-day practices, in one-hundred-degree temperatures, with twenty pounds of equipment on their backs. The coaches have to commit to twelve to fourteen-hour days of practice, watching films, nursing injuries, developing game plans, and too many other duties to list. To illustrate this, here is a sample schedule of a college football player's typical day during summer camp:

5:30 a.m. to 6:30 a.m. (affectionately referred to as the "Breakfast Club"). This hour of the morning is reserved for those players who did not show up with the needed off-season conditioning. Or they didn't run a certain time, lift the required weight, or they just generally lagged behind the others. It's a good early lesson about the need for total commitment. Some teams punish these players by making them get on their stomachs and roll the length of the football field. If you are bored sometime, see if you can do that without throwing up.

6:30 – 7:30 Breakfast

7:30 – 8:00 Position Meeting

8:00 – 10:30 Practice

10:30 – 11:00 Shower

11:00 – 12:00 Team Meeting

12:00 – 1:00 Lunch

1:00 – 2:00 Off

2:00 – 3:00 Position Meeting

3:00 – 5:30 Practice

5:30 Shower

6:00 – 7:00 Dinner

7:00 – 8:00 Team Meeting

8:00 – 9:30 Film Review

10:00 Lights Out for Players

10:00 – 12:00 midnight Coaches' Meetings

Robbie learned about commitment the hard way. Robbie was a good athlete, way above average. He excelled without having to work too hard, compared to the other kids his age. Robbie switched high schools to start his freshmen year. Without any problem he stepped right up and earned a starting position in the backfield on the football team. He had an outstanding freshmen football year. I encouraged him to lift weights, run, and get ready in the off-season for his sophomore year.

The goal of most sophomore football players—as it was for Robbie—was to play on the varsity team. Most sophomores play on the junior varsity team until they reach the eleventh grade, then they move up to varsity. If you can earn a spot on the varsity team, it is good for several reasons.

The first is, they can get on the radar of college scouts who may be at the games looking at some of the seniors on the team. A player really can't get enough exposure because college football scholarships are very hard to come by and it is a very competitive market for those who do possess the talent to play at that level. The second reason is, the experience a player gains in the 10th grade playing with juniors and seniors. That experience helps prepare the player to compete with the big boys. The third reason is, the recognition you get from your peers by sporting a varsity letterman jacket as a sophomore. Remember in high school, it's all about being the "big man on campus." There are a lot of privileges and recognition that comes with being BMOC. Gaining that coveted varsity letter in the fall of your sophomore year is also a big confidence builder for those who achieve this status.

My son had set his goal on making varsity his sophomore year. More than that, he expected to make it. Robbie didn't really train in the off-season, though. Why should he make the commitment and sacrifices when he was so good he didn't have to? He had always shown up and been the man. Why would this year be any different?

When it came time for football season, the varsity coach brought up three players from the junior varsity, Robbie and two other tenth graders. Seems Robbie's plan worked to perfection without having to go the extra mile. Robbie earned a spot on the special team's squad that year, which saw very little action on Friday nights.

Towards the end of the season, Robbie's team was way ahead in a couple of games. The coach decided to give some of the younger players a chance to gain varsity level experience. Robbie trotted out on to the field, full of piss and vinegar, ready to make his mark. The very first play, Robbie got the ball up the middle for four yards and was fighting for more. Suddenly the ball popped out. He fumbled and the other team recovered. Robbie was playing for a coach and a team where mistakes were not tolerated. Robbie was promptly pulled out of the game and did not see another play. He found out quickly that the competition at this level was much different than on the freshmen or junior-varsity team.

Robbie worked hard the next week at practice so as to get out of the coach's doghouse. The next game was the last regular season game. Robbie's team was a perennial play-off team and this year was no exception. Once again, in the last game of the regular season, Robbie's team had basically secured a win by halftime. Robbie was called into action to start the second half. It was very exciting. He was going to be able to play the entire second half! If he did well, he might get to see some action in the post-season.

In the second half, on the first play, they handed the ball off to Robbie. Up the middle he went for seven yards. He refused to go down, fighting for that extra inch, and then suddenly, out of nowhere, he fumbled the football again! This is the worst thing that could have happened besides him getting hurt. He was promptly pulled out of the game, received a chewing-out from the coach, and got to ride the pine the rest of the night.

At this point in the season, the junior varsity schedule was over. It was a tradition at this high school that the varsity coach brought up a few more JV players to reward them for a good season and to get them ready for the varsity team the next year. The play-offs in football are always full of excitement, just like in any sport. They are single elimination games so everyone brings their "A" game. They also bring the largest crowds, the most scouts, and sometimes even TV and radio coverage.

Much to Robbie's dismay, the coach pulled him into his office and told him they didn't need him for the play-offs. Robbie was crushed, confused, mad, and hurt all at once. Just because he fumbled a couple of times he was not going to get the chance to dress for the play-offs? His season was over just like that? Was it because Robbie fumbled or because he didn't make the proper level of commitment in order to play at the varsity level in the off-season? He didn't know, but he did know his season was over.

This was a pretty tough lesson to learn. Robbie went to the coaches to plead his case, but no luck. I contemplated getting involved, to understand why the coach had made this decision, but in the end I decided it was be better to leave it alone. Hopefully it would be a learning experience for Robbie.

So my son was a spectator watching his team in the playoffs. The team did well, but fell one game short of the state championship. None of the other J.V. kids saw any action in the playoffs. They did not get in for even one play. They did get the experience and thrill of being part of the team, though.

The last significant event of that season was the annual football banquet. It's a time to reflect on the season as well as hand out awards and varsity letters. During the season Robbie had been in more plays on the varsity team than any other sophomore, with the exception of one teammate who was also a sophomore. When it came time to hand out the letters, every one of the other J.V. players who were called up at the end of the season— even though they were only called up for four games and were not involved in a single play— all received a varsity letter! When Robbie's name was called, he received a J.V. certificate. How do you think he felt about this? Do you think this was fair? Now that you have answered that in your mind, do you think life is always fair? I think most of you would have answered no, life is not always fair. This was a pretty tough way for a young man to learn about commitment.

This situation could have been one of those potential turning points in a person's life. It was certainly a test of character. Robbie could have gotten very mad and reacted by quitting football altogether. He could have walked around saying how the coach screwed him and singled him out. Based on the circumstances either one of those would have been somewhat justified. But Robbie didn't do either of these things.

One day, a few weeks later, I walked by his room and saw his J.V. Certificate pinned to his wall over all his trophies for swimming, running, and various other accomplishments. There was something written in black magic marker on the certificate. When I looked closer, I read the words Robbie had written in big letters, "Those who fail to prepare, prepare to fail." Benjamin Franklin first wrote these words and they rang true for my son two hundred years later. Robbie wrote this on his JV certificate to remind him of the feeling he had when he was not called up for his varsity letter. He and I had never talked about what those words meant. I was proud that he understood them, and that he'd learned a very valuable lesson—one that transcends the game. I felt badly for Robbie, knowing how much that hurt him, but a little pain for a lifetime of gain was worth it.

Robbie handled his situation with courage and dignity. This might not seem like such a big thing to you, but remember being in high school and being an athlete, this was a very big deal. Robbie put the certificate in a place where he saw it every day as a reminder of what he needed to do to achieve his goals for the following season.

BONA FIDE

Having a bona fide commitment is absolutely one of the key attributes to success in both a person's personal and professional life. A commitment almost always involves some level of sacrifice and time. I'm positive that many of the football players that commit to the grueling summer schedule would much rather be chasing girls, staying up late, playing video games, and sleeping in.

Let's see, you can do all those fun things or wear twenty pounds of equipment in the ninty-degree heat, with coaches yelling at you, and guys trying to knock you off your feet. Football players learn early on about real commitment.

Of course you have to make some level of commit to succeed in any sport. You don't even have to play sports to learn about commitment. The people who are flipping burgers have to make a different kind of commitment. They have to commit to show up on time and execute their job responsibilities. Like I said, there are different levels of commitment. The earlier in life you understand how to totally commit to something, the more success you will enjoy.

There are many people in the world today who are just "going through the motions." They are not committed to their families, their careers, and, even more unfortunately, they are not committed to themselves. This is obvious as I review all the resumes that come across my desk regularly. In my career I have reviewed thousands of resumes and interviewed hundreds of people, mostly in sales and management.

Some people switch jobs once every year or so. Each time there seems to be a very justifiable reason for the change. In my opinion, the only legitimate reason to switch jobs is something changed dramatically that either stifled their growth or their earnings opportunities. If it is a pattern, the real reasons are they didn't do their due diligence upfront when investigating the job, or they had no commitment to the new opportunity to begin with. I am perfectly aware that, in this economy, companies go out of business, downsize, etc. Again, a prudent businessperson should see some of these signs going into a new opportunity and thus certainly try to avoid this as a career pattern.

When I interview people for my sales education/speaking company (www. SalesBuilders.com) for the clients that we work with, we try to test the candidate's commitment. One of our standard interviewing questions is, "What do you do best?" Everybody is quick and well rehearsed for that question. The follow up question is, "What do you need to do better?" The candidate usually pauses and some are bold enough to say, "nothing." That's the wrong answer and is not acceptable. So we sit there until they come up with something. There's not a person in this universe who can't improve on something. Finally I get an answer. Frequently it's something like, "I need to be more organized, I need to be more patient, etc." Great, now we are getting somewhere.

The truth is, I'm not really very interested in what they think they need to improve upon. It's the response to the next question that really counts: "So now that you have told me you need to improve in (whatever area they told me), tell me two or three things you have done recently to address this situation to better yourself." Most people look like a deer caught in the headlights when I ask this one. Why? Because the honest answer is that most of them have done nothing about it. Not one thing. They have no commitment to change or improve. If a person is not always striving to better themselves on a regular basis, they are most likely just getting by or coasting through life. That's why I think so many people switch jobs as often as they do.

When you start a new job there is a "honeymoon period." Most people accept and pursue jobs they think they will have some level of success with. Once it starts getting a little harder or maybe the company loses their competitive edge (which all companies do at some point), they look for the next wave to ride, i.e. a new job. Instead of trying to better themselves, learn new skills, learn more about the market, build a better network, etc. they just jump ship for the next ride. There is no commitment. There is a saying, "you are either green and growing or ripe and dying." Complacency is a big issue in our work force today for both individuals and companies. As soon as you get comfortable, you are in for some rough times. There is always someone out there on your heels. The markets are too volatile and competitive to ever rest on your laurels.

In football you can't get away with that type of mentality. You get too comfortable on the field and someone will knock your head off. You get too comfortable as a player and there is someone right behind you dying to take your spot. In order to excel in football or even just survive, players must always work hard to improve themselves. Whether it is in the weight room trying to get stronger, on the track trying to get faster, or looking at films trying to better execute their assignments. The bottom line is, they have to continuously improve. You get complacent as a team and you will lose. Get complacent as a player and you'll be replaced. There is no honeymoon for football players!

Earlier this year I interviewed a young man who played for the Denver Broncos for three years. Being an ex-pro football player made his resume stand out in a big way. I knew if he understood the secret of football he would be very successful in the job he was seeking. To my surprise, during my interview with the ex-player, as we were discussing his career and the reasons why he wasn't still playing, he educated me on just how committed the players had to be and how complacency can't exist in the make-up of a successful NFL player. Here's how: the players go through a summer camp schedule similar to the college player's summer schedule I detailed for you earlier. NFL teams are only allowed to carry a certain number of players so every few days they cut their roster down based on their needs and the skill sets of the players. You can bet there is no complacency in these camps! It is probably the most intense time of any player's life.

Let's say you worked hard in the off-season, the coaches see your commitment, they have a need for your skills, and you make the team. There was a cable show a few years back called *Inside the Baltimore Ravens* and the following year it was *Inside the Dallas Cowboys*. The HBO crew had unprecedented access to the teams, the coaches, the team meetings, the locker room, everything. It allowed us all to see how the coaches made their decisions about who to keep and who to cut. You could see the emotional roller coaster the players went through. Every week they showed us at least one player who snuck out of camp in the middle of the night because he couldn't take it—no commitment. The show followed a few players every week and you could almost feel the same anxiety they felt. The last show ended with the final roster of guys who made the team.

In college, when they offer you a scholarship, you are guaranteed that scholarship for at least that year. Most people, myself included, thought the NFL worked the same way, especially considering the contract process the players, agents, and teams go through. I was shocked to discover it doesn't work that way at all.

The bulk of the players have a game-by-game contract. Tuesdays are the player's day off and every Tuesday the coaches bring in new players for tryouts. If they think another player can perform better than a current player on the team, the new guy joins the team and the existing player is cut from the roster. If a player continues to stay on the team for three games they are guaranteed 50 percent of their contract. Every Wednesday when the players come to practice the first thing they do is check the team roster to make sure they are still a member of the team. So, in essence, if a player isn't giving 100 percent, executing their responsibilities, and performing at the top of their game, then they are replaced. There is no time or patience for complacency or lack of commitment.

To finish the interview story, this young man had been on the Broncos for three years. One Wednesday he checked the roster and his name was not on the list. Another player had replaced him. He had no prospects for another job and of course he hadn't been looking. A player can't really interview with other teams, especially during the season. He was a professional football player and that was his job. Looking for a job outside the field of football never even entered his mind. He had to pick up and start all over the day he was replaced.

I'd say the way the NFL works is pretty brutal and heartless. The teams really don't have a choice, though. If a team doesn't do well, there are lots of changes made, from the coaches on down. The owner, fans, and media all expect the team to win. They demand results and the only acceptable result is winning. It's a little different in college and high school football, but not much. As soon as you get complacent or show a lack of commitment, there is someone right behind you ready to step up and take your position. You may not be cut from the team, but you will wind up on the bench, "riding the pine."

If the company you worked for operated this same way, would you act differently in how you approach your day-to-day job responsibilities? My guess is you answered yes. That would be the honest answer for most of us, but it is the wrong viewpoint. If we all applied the same level of commitment to our jobs that an NFL player does, we would all be much more successful. Fear is a powerful motivator, but if you are 100 percent committed and always striving to improve, ensuring complacency never sets in, you have nothing to fear because you will perform and receive the desired (and required) results.

Regardless of whether it is your career, personal relationships, or football, there is an absolute correlation between your success and your level of commitment. We all need to be aware of this and measure our commitment on a regular basis. If you are not committed, then you will not achieve the results you want. The young men who play football understand and learn this concept early in their lives. If they apply the same level of commitment when they played the game of football to all aspects of their lives after football, they will prosper in all aspects of their lives and in the endeavors they pursue.

Now, if you really understand and decide to do what you've read about in this chapter, you just might carry the ball over the goal line toward your own life's goals.

CHAPTER THREE

BEFORE THE SNAP
DISCIPLINE AND SETTING GOALS

If you believe in yourself, have the courage, the determination, the dedication, the competitive drive, and if you are willing to sacrifice the little things in life to pay the price for the things that are worthwhile, it can be done.

COACH VINCE LOMBARDI

In chapter 2, we discussed commitment and dedication as an example of the typical football player's day during summer camp. These athletes are focused on achieving a result and they work as hard as needed to achieve it. They possess a "whatever it takes attitude."

Raw talent only goes so far. However, hard work can make up for a lot of shortcomings. In my career in management, I would much rather have dedicated, hard workers who are less talented, than someone who is talented but doesn't work as hard. The person with lots of talent and less work ethic in the long run will be less productive than the harder worker. It's a different version of the tortoise and the hare story. The tortoise will keep moving along, working hard and, more than likely, pass the hare. Hard work never hurt anyone. Like Mark Twain said, "Don't go around saying the world owes you a living. The world owes you nothing. It was here first."

We all develop work habits early in our lives and have several positive and negative reinforcements that help form our work ethic as we mature. Any child who is asked to perform a chore and takes their sweet 'ole time in getting it done or does the job poorly just to get it finished is likely to develop a poor work ethic—unless there are consequences for their actions. The same is true for the child who does a great job the first time and is praised and rewarded for their efforts. Isn't this how the real world operates? If we do a great job we get rewarded with a pay raise or a promotion. The other side of the coin is just as true: You do a poor job, you're lazy, or you have a poor work ethic and don't achieve the required results—you're terminated.

All of the most popular sports demand an ever-increasing work ethic. When I participated in athletics in my youth, it was not unusual to play two or three different sports. It gave me variety throughout the year, and I could be very competitive in all of them. Today, the serious athletes have to pretty much dedicate themselves to one sport if they want to play at the college level. Today's required work ethic is extreme. I know many kids who start practice for ice hockey, tennis, and weight training at 5:00 a.m. several days a week. Baseball has become a year-round sport for players by the age of nine or ten. Once the regular season is over, older kids join traveling teams and play nearly ten months out of the year. The kids who don't play fall way behind in growth, experience, and needed skills. Basketball is very similar. They have summer leagues that get the kids ready and finely tuned for the winter schedule.

Football, in my opinion, has the most demanding work ethic of any sport. Players as young as thirteen play a full schedule during the fall football season, plus spring football, and then an additional four more weeks in the summer. And they should be running and lifting all winter.

In college football, there are required summer, fall, and spring workout schedules. The other times of the year are optional. Right. Optional. On most college teams, if you are not working out with the team in an "unofficial" capacity, you will likely not see much playing time during the season. Even if the program one is playing in does not have this unwritten rule, the players still have to run and lift weights just to stay competitive for the coming season. The fact is, football is a year-round sport.

When Robbie started high school, he had about the same level of talent and skill in both baseball and football. He was one of the fastest players on the baseball team. He could almost always stretch a single into extra bases. He also had a great arm and could throw a player out from almost anywhere on the field. His high school baseball team was always competing in the state championship tournament and won it several times. After the season, the players went right into a summer and fall program.

By his sophomore year, Robbie had to choose between football and baseball. He could have gone far in either sport, but he chose football. Robbie had two teammates who were actually able to play both baseball and football in their senior year. Since the football season ends first, both of these young men were offered football scholarships to Division I universities.

One of their decision points for which offer they would accept was whether or not they would be allowed to play baseball in addition to playing football. As they went through the recruiting processes, the colleges courting them said that they could play both sports. One player went to the University of Louisville and the other to the University of North Carolina, Chapel Hill. Once they completed their first season of football, they both realized there was no way they could also play baseball. The work ethic required for football forced each of them to dedicate themselves to that sport alone.

It would have been nice to see how far these kids could have gone in baseball, but in the world outside of sports we usually have to dedicate ourselves to one profession, too. There are not many doctors, accountants, or lawyers who work part of the time in these professions and also work as a salesperson, stockbroker, or truck driver the rest of the year. It takes a laser-like focus and dedicated work ethic to succeed in one profession, let alone two. So, the demand that is put on kids by the ninth or tenth grade to focus on one sport alone is just another microcosmic reflection of the world outside of sports.

Most of us do not play sports for more than a short time. Football, at the professional level, only lasts a very short time. Even though players have played from as young as six up to their mid-thirties, they need to learn the secret of football so they can apply this knowledge to the rest of the world outside of sports. Some players continue playing to the age of forty, but the majority end their careers in their late twenties and early thirties. This leaves them a long time to live and do well outside of the game of football.

So how does one do well? The answer begins with *discipline*.

There are too many times the end results we seek and the actions we follow do not line up. Many people talk a good game, but they often don't follow through. Certainly none of you reading this book are guilty, but have you ever witnessed someone who is doing his or her job just well enough to get by? These typically are the people who loaf the most and the same ones who complain the most about where they are in their lives. The results they want to achieve and the actions they follow, especially in the area of work ethic, are in conflict with each other. Activities like leaving early whenever they can, making the numbers and then coasting, learning and applying the minimum, are just a few of the thousand things that most people are guilty of from time to time. That's fine as long as you want to put your time in, do okay, retire at sixty-five-years old, and live off Social Security, provided it is still around. I have yet to meet a person who told me this was their plan. On the other hand, I rarely meet people who have a well thought out plan for success.

Have you ever met a consistently successful person who didn't follow a disciplined routine? Making it up as you go along is not a good plan. It will not take you to the destination you are seeking. A disciplined routine starts early in sports and should transcend regardless of what your future life pursuits are. Football players all follow disciplined routines consistently regardless of the level they play—from high school to the NFL. Let's face it: You can't lift weights every now and then and have the strength required to compete with the vast majority of players who do follow disciplined daily routines. The same is true with running, stretching, and every other part of the game. You have to have a plan and a disciplined routine.

How many times have you heard someone say they're going to lose ten pounds? Most of us would like to lose ten pounds. The first question is: how? The answer that usually comes back is, "I'm going to diet."

"Okay, what do you mean by diet?"

"Oh, I'm going to eat less and drink less beer."

If you were a betting person, how much would you wager on this person being successful in their quest to lose ten pounds? Save your money. They are not going to succeed.

A disciplined person answers the question this way: "I am going to only eat fifteen hundred calories a day, eat no bread, eat nothing after 8:00 pm, go to the gym for a one hour weight workout on Mondays, Wednesdays and Fridays and run for forty-five minutes on the other days."

This person will succeed if they commit to this routine and will measure their progress along the way

There are all kinds of clever sayings that make this point. You might be familiar with: "Plan your work and work your plan." One of the concepts we go into in some detail in my company's *Quid Pro Quo* training courses is the importance of work ethic and working a plan. We focus on a time-tested formula that applies to all of us: Activity times Time equals Results.

This formula is universal. It works for athletes and non-athletes alike. The basic foundation is that the activities you choose to pursue and the time you spend on that activity will, in the end, determine the results you will achieve. This is a simple concept, but it is amazing how much time and energy we need to spend teaching this to people. Equally amazing is that, more often than not, we have to go back to hold additional workshops to review the details over and over.

There are only so many hours in a day. We must choose how we spend them wisely. If a football player wants to be a superstar athlete but spends a good portion of his time playing video games, his activity is counter to his goal. If the same person is in the gym or trying in some way to further their skills, then they are helping themselves obtain their ultimate goal.

This is not rocket science. Let's see how it applies to the workaday world.

For this example let's say you make your living selling—like many people do. Let's look at your activity. There are 256 working days (365 days in a year minus 104 weekend days minus five days of vacation equals 256 days) in a calendar year. One of the keys to success in sales, or any business for that matter, is finding and acquiring new customers. In most businesses you can't just hang out your shingle and hope people rush to break down your door to do business with you. It's a great concept, but it rarely happens that way. Most of us have to follow a proactive plan of pursuing and creating opportunities.

In this example you are selling a product that costs $50,000 and your sales quota is $1,000,000 in a twelve-month period. As a new account salesperson you have to make outbound calls to prospective clients. This is called "cold calling." There are not too many sales people who are fond of this activity and there is typically a great deal of call reluctance that exists in all sales people. No one wants to be perceived as the person calling during dinner hour, trying to sell long distance services, siding for your house, time-shares, or a host of other absolutely non-critical items.

Most sales people need to be trained on creating the right perception that results in cold-calling productivity. All the details about this are in my book called *Mutual Respect*.

Here are two simple examples of how to apply discipline to "cold calling" activity:

1) Make a commitment to put in two extra calls a day. That is 512 additional calls a year (256 working days times two extra calls a day).

2) Make a commitment to ask every cold call for a referral. The conversation goes like this, "I understand you do not have a need for (my product), but I would really appreciate it if you could help me. Can you please tell me someone you know who might have a need for (my product) at this time." The reasoning for this is simple: referrals are the best way not to sound like the telemarketer salesperson calling during dinner. Besides, referrals

make the best prospects and they tend to buy more times than not. It is also human nature to want to help someone who asks. So now you have an activity with a workable approach. You also have to be committed to put time towards this activity.

Let's say at the beginning you receive a referral only 10 percent of the time. That equals fifty-one referrals in the course of a year. (256 working days times two extra calls a day times 10 percent success). You now have fifty-one new prospects to pursue as referrals simply by making two extra calls a day and *always* asking for referrals.

The final part of the formula is the results portion. Again you can plug the numbers in, but the closing percentage for a referral versus a cold call is dramatically higher. Let's say you successfully close 20 percent of the referrals you receive. Using the same calculations, that means you sold or closed 10.5 new accounts (20 percent of the fifty-one referrals). We have already established that the average selling price is $50,000, so 10.5 new accounts from our disciplined routine of making just two extra calls a day and asking for referrals has earned you sales of $525,000. That's $525,000 of new business you would not have created if you didn't have the work ethic to make the two extra calls and the discipline to ask for a referral every time. This one activity has now accounted for more than half of your annual quota!

Good work! Call me if you need a job!

This formula (Activity times Time equals Results) applies to almost all professions. Doctors, lawyers, accountants, stockbrokers, real-estate professionals, etc., all need to generate more clients consistently. More clients mean more business. To obtain more clients, you have to have an activity with time dedicated to that activity. That is the way to achieve results.

Another way to look at this formula is by applying a slightly different approach—one that applies to everyone who is in the profession of earning money. (and who isn't?) Figure out how much money you would like to earn in a twelve-month period. This example works best if you have some percentage of your income that is variable or if you are in business for yourself. One of my business principles says whether you are working for a company or not, we are all in business for ourselves, or should be. For the ease of calculating let's say you want to earn at least $100,000 in a twelve-month period. Now break that $100,000 down by the day. (256 working days divided by $100,000 equals $391 per working day.) That's what you will have to earn to achieve your $100,000 goal. But let's not stop there. Let's break it down to the hour. You work eight hours a day. That means you are earning or are worth $49 an hour.

If you use this number to govern your activities you might find yourself applying your time differently. So when you think of playing golf during the week with a client you have to figure not only the cost of the round of golf, but also what it will cost you in time. The same is true for that extended lunch, or all the personal activities during the time you could or should be pursuing earning opportunities. It takes true discipline to think this way, but if you can, it will instill a new level of work ethic in you and give you better results. The math of this formula, just like the one above, is undisputable. The closer you can adhere to these ideas, the closer you will get to achieving and exceeding your goals.

Another real concept to consider in the quest to earn the success you desire would be to add one extra hour daily to your working routine. What if you committed to working just one extra hour a day, sixty additional minutes of productive time? How much do you think that would improve your results?

There are many examples we could use, one being a book-writing example. I'm slightly dyslexic. Okay, a *lot* dyslexic. Let's put it this way, it's a good thing my name is Bob. That way if I reverse the letters, I can still at least spell my name right! So it might take me thirty minutes to write one page, two pages in an hour. If I spend just five hours a week writing only two pages a day, in one hudred days (three months, ten days), I will have finished a book. If you're not dyslexic and you have a disciplined plan and the work ethic to execute it, look how quickly you could finish a book. If you don't want to write a book, consider what you *do* want to accomplish—like maybe losing ten pounds? The same principle and math apply. If you start exercising one hour each day over a period of a year, you would have exercised the equivalent of more than fifteen complete days!

Apply this concept to your current career. By working one extra hour each day, you extend your year of productive time by over six weeks (one hour times 365 days divided by eight hours in a workday)! I can't tell you how many times I would have liked to have extended my year by six weeks. I would have never missed my revenue commitments. It all starts with a dedicated work ethic.

Hard work is always recognized and is usually rewarded. Most managers will tell you that if a person is working hard, willing to learn, and giving their all, but still not getting the required results, they will tend to stick with that person a little longer in order to help them succeed. It is easier to want to help those people who are dedicated and have an unparalleled work ethic. Everyone pulls for this person and, given the right direction, that person will more often succeed.

One story that comes to mind is about Steve Hughes, an ex-football player from the University of Wisconsin who worked for a consulting company as a sales person. Steve was not making his quota. No matter how hard he tried, he was not able to achieve the required results. He also worked for a small company. This group could not afford to invest in a low-productivity sales person. Every person in this organization made a significant impact. As such, every employee was either part of solution or part of the problem.

I was brought in to consult with this company, to help them achieve a new level of success. By the time I started consulting for this company, Steve was labeled as part of the problem. The thing about Steve was that he worked harder than anyone else. He really wanted to succeed and was committed to doing whatever it took. With his attitude, personality, and will to succeed, everyone liked him. Steve already had been designated to be replaced; however, his work ethic just could not be overlooked.

A long story made short: Steve's work ethic bought him the time he needed to figure it out. With the proper guidance and some personal coaching Steve started to show the necessary results. Steve must have learned the secret of football during his time at Wisconsin because he applied almost all of that principle in his struggle to succeed with this company. In the course of one year, Steve went from being marked for replacement to the company's #1 sales person! Last time I checked on Steve, he was still his company's #1 sales person year in and year out.

LUCKY

The best definition of luck I know: luck is where preparation and opportunity meet. To give luck a chance, one needs to capitalize on opportunities that put oneself in a situation where favorable developments can occur. And if they don't exist there, create them. We can, indeed, create our own luck.

Do you really think it is luck when a fullback makes a deceptive move and—as the defender slips—he runs past them for a touchdown? The defensive side of the house might brush it off as their bad luck or the fullback's good luck; however, more often than not there is not much luck involved. Fullbacks practice footwork for hours, running through the bungee cord obstacle course. They work on head fakes and spin moves, so luck doesn't have a whole lot to do with the defender slipping. The fullback caused him to slip. He made his own luck.

To be fair to the defensive side of the ball, the same is also true. How many times have you seen a defender intercept a pass and think it was lucky? You might think the quarterback threw the ball right to them. Guess what. Quarterbacks at all levels are smart enough to recognize different color jerseys and would not be quarterbacks if they weren't proficient at passing. Again, it is not a matter of luck. The defenders put themselves in the position to make the play. Either they read the route of the receiver, followed the quarterback's eyes or made up a lot of ground between the time the quarterback passed the ball and the time the ball got to the receiver. The point is, they worked hard watching films, running, and a host of other activities, to put themselves in a position to be where the ball was thrown. Tremendous preparation goes into every aspect of the game.

Almost all sports require more preparation than meets the eye. Things that look effortless on the surface are anything but. A lot of time and preparation goes into creating that effortless look.

How would you grade yourself in preparing and taking regular action to achieve the success you want? For example: before you contact a prospect or go on a sales call have you considered doing some research? A few facts to collect might include researching the person you are working with. Some areas of their background you might want to find out about are:

- School
- Family
- Years at the company
- Hobbies
- Where they worked before
- Stresses at work

Then you would further help yourself by researching his company:

- Line of business
- Latest results
- Competitors
- Latest trends
- Business initiatives

Then the company's political environment:

- Who has what title?
- Who works for whom?
- Who has the real power?
- Are there any competing personal agendas?
- Who has what tenure?

Then you would do well to explore the current needs:

- Is there a pressing reason they are considering working with you at this time?
- What is the budget?
- What is their decision process?
- What's the time frame to make a decision?
- Who is involved in the decision-making process?

As I said earlier, the preparation process goes deep. Football players learn this very early in the game. Sure it takes more effort to do your homework up front. The work ethic you apply to this is the difference between being "lucky" or not.

One of the things I never said to my son before any of his football games was "good luck." He didn't need good luck to perform at an exceptional level. He had worked his butt off year after year and was in a position to make greats things happen. Wishing him good luck before a game was like saying "good luck" to someone in a poker game when they are holding four aces. My son already held the winning hand. All he had to do was execute like he had practiced and prepared.

Some people have a tendency to use luck as an excuse for failure. They portray themselves as victims of circumstance when things don't go the way they want them to. They use this instead of recognizing inadequacies of skill or effort! If someone runs into what appears to be a string of bad luck, they would be ill-advised to retreat into a hole, thinking "the world is against me." At the end of the day, we all make our own luck! This even applies to the person who wins the lottery too. They had to go spend the money and buy the ticket to win. Be honest, have you ever thought to yourself, "I sure would like to win the lottery," but you haven't even bought a ticket. What is even more frustrating is when you hear someone say "I wish." I wish I would have started that company; I wish I would have bought that piece of property; I wish I was in that kind of shape. These are all things you have the power to make happen. There's no luck needed, just a dedicated work ethic and follow through. The only sure thing about luck is, it will only change when *you* are ready to change. Your "luck" is determined when you take control. Luck knows no limits, only people do.

Robbie created his own luck. He had an unwavering routine and work ethic to achieve his goal. He learned early in life through his football experiences that the only way to insure he got something was to work for it. His typical after-school routine was to run with a trainer and then go to the gym to lift weights. The running entailed running with a parachute, running with bungee cords, and a host of other apparatuses as resistance exercises to increase his speed.

One day, the trainer forgot all the equipment for running so he suggested that they just go to the gym and lift. Robbie wanted nothing to do with that and told the trainer he knew where he could run. He took the trainer to a vacant parking lot. Next to the lot was a hill that went straight up for about sixty yards. Robbie ran the hill that day until he was nearly sick. Then he went to the gym. His trainer later told me that 99.9 percent of the kids he'd worked with would have taken the day off from running, but not Robbie. Robbie went on to be selected as most dedicated player on his high school team. His work ethic and dedication helped him get a "lucky" scholarship to one of the best universities in the county. Boy, that Robbie. He's lucky! He'll be really "lucky" if he brings that same dedication and work ethic to whatever he chooses to pursue in the fifth quarter, after his football career ends.

As you reflect on this chapter on work ethic and luck, can you think of anything you can do tomorrow (or better yet today) that might improve your "luck"?

Read on because what I'm about to tell you will provide you astonishing power to help answer that question.

It's called a *goal*.

THE GOAL LINE

The goal line in football is similar to goals we all strive for in life. **A goal is an ongoing pursuit of an objective until it is accomplished. It is a person's road map. Whatever you desire in life**: buckets of money, the love of your life, a new home, a new body, a successful career, a fresh start, the awe and respect of people who now doubt you, **it all can be attained through the astonishing power of goal-setting.**

Define where the goal line is for you and work toward crossing that line, no matter what. It doesn't matter where you've been in life or even where you are right now. It doesn't matter if you played football or never even participated in a sport. Your future starts as soon as you establish your goals. The past is behind you. Whether it was good or bad with regard to your accomplishments, it doesn't matter. **The only thing that matters is where you're going from here.** Don't think for a second that your background or education matters. It doesn't. Neither does talent, skill, ability, age, current situation, knowledge, or pure dumb luck. **The only thing keeping you from the life you want to live is you.**

Every football team and player sets goals. It is just as much part of the game as the forward pass. Of course, goals have to be deeper and stated in more detail than "we want to win." That's a worthwhile goal and every team has that objective. The other requirement is the "how" part, the specific details of the goal. The best analogy is someone who has the desire to run a marathon.

If someone told you that they wanted to run a marathon but never exercised and is thirty pounds overweight, your first thought might be "how?" You don't see any chance of them running 26.2 miles. Now, if they told you in detail of a new exercise routine, how many miles a week they were planning to run, their cross-training routines and the time frames associated with the plan, you might begin to believe they were serious about their goals. Whether you are a football player or a parking lot attendant, you need to set your goals and commit to the detailed activities you will have to perform and the time frames associated to achieve each one.

Some people set goals because they heard somewhere along the way it was a good thing to do. That's good, but it's not enough. Without sincere intention and follow-through there's no sense in going through the motions of setting goals. When you have a clear vision and a burning desire, then you can achieve whatever you put your mind to.

Imagine waking up every morning full of energy, springing out of bed, and looking forward to what the day has in store for you. Imagine feeling totally focused, fully knowing that you are on your way toward getting what you want. Imagine having the constant feeling that you just can't wait to get on with things, each day filled with happiness and passion. Imagine living the life that you choose. Imagine your business running like clockwork, taking you closer and closer to your dreams. Imagine never having to find the time to do things because you love what you do. Imagine feeling totally successful and reaping the rewards of a highly successful person: materially, physically, emotionally, and spiritually.

So my question to you is: do you have a clear burning desire vision for your life and your career? One thing is certain, you can have whatever you can imagine and are willing to work for. But it all starts with your goals.

Most of the population, though, will do nothing to change their circumstances or create the situations they desire. They may complain, but most make no changes. Most continue to live in la-la-land, unhappy enough to complain, but not happily living the life of their dreams either. Are you one of them? Let's make sure you aren't.

Here's how to visualize and achieve your burning desire:

1. Start at the Beginning: One of the hardest parts about goal setting is determining what you want. Even many football players struggle with being detailed enough when they set their goals. At this point there are no limits; nothing is out of the question or out of bounds. Go for it, whatever "it" is. Goal setting does require some effort on your part though so be prepared to do some work. Your first assignment is to grab a piece of paper and a pencil. Okay, now that you have your

tools, start writing. Make a list of everything you would like to have happen, everything you would like to acquire, every possible thing you can think of. After you have exhausted your "want list," organize them by priority from those that are most important to you to those that are the least important.

2. No Passengers: Once again, review this list to be sure everything you have written on your list is *your* desire, *your* goals. Make sure that no one on your bus is whispering things in your ear. Ensure that *their* goals are not added to your list. There is no room for baggage on this trip, no passengers either. It is easy to let people influence you on what you think you want. Don't let society, your parents, your spouse, your friends, or anyone else set the bar of success for you. It will absolutely be either too high or too low. You are the only one that can set the bar just where it needs to be.

3. Details Count: There are three essential ingredients in goal setting. The first is "Be specific." "Specific" means defining what you want to have. Next, include all the steps you have to do in order to get what you want. Then, set the time targets you'll need in order to complete each step. When are you going to achieve your goals? There are no unrealistic goals, just unrealistic time frames. Keep that thought in mind as you develop your plan. If you say your goal is to earn $150,000 in one year sometime after getting out of school, that would be almost pointless. It might have taken you thirty years if there was no time frame associated with the goal. So would it be worth claiming victory if thirty years before, you had set the bar so low

that an ant could have jumped over it? What would have been the point?

THE SECOND INGREDIENT IS: Your goals should be worthwhile and big. If they aren't, again, what's the point? If your goal is to get out of bed every morning and you attain that by getting up every morning, don't waste your time setting goals. I know that's not you or you wouldn't be reading this book. Extend your reach and try to achieve just a little more than you might think you may be capable of. You might surprise yourself and a whole lot of other people. Just like everything worthwhile, you have to push yourself. If you make sure your goals are far-reaching and challenging enough, it will be a lot harder for you to become complacent and satisfied with your current situation. You should never be satisfied with anything less than achieving 100 percent of your goals. But don't always set your goals so low that you always achieve them. At the end of the day, you want to be able to look back and see all the ground you have covered. It should be very meaningful to you. Think big, think often, and think about your goals all the time. Then you will see how far you can really stretch.

THE THIRD INGREDIENT: What I'm about to say now might seem to be a little bit of a mixed message: And that is, be realistic. Although nothing is out of bounds in setting your goals, you will still need to apply common sense to the process. If you are five-foot-two-inches and 125 pounds and never played football in your life, a goal of being starting linebacker for an NFL team in the Super Bowl is probably not in the cards. A little dose of reality can go a long way in getting better results. "Realistic" is one of those misunderstood words. What is realistic to you and what is realistic to someone else can be very different. When you set a goal, just remember that you are going to need a time-frame and a well thought-out plan on how to achieve it. Our five-foot-two-inch warrior who is ready to go rip someone's head off is more likely to jump on someone's back and go for a ride on the football field. What I would be interested in seeing is the detail on how he plans to become a foot taller, add one hundred pounds, and acquire the skills and talent needed since he has never played before. Maybe he can put a plan together that will achieve those things, but it's a long shot and the energy spent trying could be better used in another, more obtainable goal. Sometimes people do achieve seemingly impossible goals. But is he being realistic?

Whatever your goals are—just like a good football player—they need to have balance. We will discuss this further, but for now let's agree your overall goals and plans must have several different parts to make them work. It can't be just about the pursuit of material objects or career objectives. You have to take into account your health, your leisure time, family time, time for your friends and associates, your community, your church, and the world you live in. You will never go to the graveyard and see a headstone that says, "If I only had spent more time at the office." For you to achieve your goals you have to achieve a balance in your life.

There is a common saying, "You get back what you give off." Simplified, it means that you have to give in order to get. My wife tells me that all the time. You can't be totally absorbed with yourself and think you will achieve your full potential.

It took me a long time to understand this. I was fortunate to be in the presence of some successful ex-professional football players and business executives very early in my career. I always asked them their secret to success, and they all had a common theme. They all gave of their time, talent, and money to serve others. Every time I heard them say that, it only frustrated me. I was working my butt off! I didn't have any time and I was having a hard enough time trying to build my family's own fortune, let alone give time and money away!

In executive management, a lot of my pay was incentive-based. If I achieved certain goals, I earned commissions and bonuses. My focus and goals were crystal clear: Earn the most I could. This just happened to be right in line with the company's goals. I did very well and usually was the highest paid person in the company. I also made the biggest contribution. It wasn't until I started my own company that the concept of *donation* sank in. My company, Sales Builders Inc., is focused on helping people and organizations become more productive. We offer our customers new sales approaches, tools, workshops, and consulting. The purpose is really based on helping other people first, everything else is secondary.

The most amazing thing happened through this process. By focusing on other people first and helping them to achieve better results, my work has become extremely rewarding and satisfying. Also, the money is better than ever before. The priorities are lined up and the rewards naturally follow. I only wish this epiphany had sunk in years earlier.

Finally, you have to write down your goals for them to be meaningful. Do this in the form of a contract. When you write a contract, you will think about it in more detail, and more analytically. You wouldn't welch on a contract with yourself, would you? You should write it out in contract form and even sign it! I know it sounds silly, but signing it furthers your commitment to you.

So your goal checklist is:

1. Determine what you want. Write an unlimited list of things down.

2. Prioritize the list.

3. Assess the list and make sure it is indeed your list.

4. Make sure you have specific steps to take and that each step has a realistic time target.

5. Create far-reaching and big goals. Push yourself.

6. Assure you have balance. Consider all aspects of your life.

7. Think of others and give back.

8. Write it up as a contract and sign your contract.

Don't get discouraged.

This might be your first time setting goals, or maybe you have done it before and weren't as committed or as ready as you are now. Goal setting is not a natural activity for anyone. It is a learned discipline just like so many other things. If at first you don't succeed, try, try again. We have all heard that before, probably when you were a young child. As adults we need to take it to heart more than ever.

Did you know that **Michael Jordan** was cut from his high school basketball team? **Arnold Schwarzenegger** was told he'd never make it in Hollywood. **Thomas Edison** had a sixth-grade education and **Sam Walton** (Wal-Mart) was considered too much of a hillbilly to ever accomplish anything. **Jim Carey, the world-famous actor and comedian, was once homeless, living in the back of a van.** But to him, it didn't matter where he was, only where he was going. He relentlessly pursued his dreams through the practice of goal-setting and today earns over twenty million dollars per film. From homeless to twenty million dollars a movie, now that is some goal! You see, it didn't matter to these people where they were, only where they were going. They give credit for their achievements to goal-setting—and acting on those goals—as the driving force that helped them realize their dreams.

Your next step, once you have prioritized your goals, is to organize them into different categories. You want to use the exact formula we established in the previous pages. You have to be specific regarding each step you have to do, and each step needs a time target.

The chart below is a suggestion of possible categories for you to consider.

GOAL AREAS:

Health & Fitness Goals

    Exercise, Nutrition, Weight-Loss, Peak Performance

Family & Relationship Goals

    Friends, Romance, Family, People Skills, Family Goals

Career Goals

    Job Seeking, Education & Skills, College & Grad School, Job Related, K-12, Languages, Technical Literacy, Entrepreneurship, Promotions

Time Management & Organization Goals

    Record keeping, Housekeeping

Personal Finance and Asset Goals

    Investing, Paying off Debt, Cutting Expenses, and Charity

Home Improvement & Real Estate Goals

    Investing, Additions, Selling

Personal Growth & Interest Goals

    Arts, Music, Writing, Community, Spirituality

Recreation & Leisure Goals

    Travel, Boating, Golf, Outdoors, Cooking, Vacation

As you establish your goals in each of these areas make sure:

- You are absolutely clear on what you want.
- You know how your career goal fits with your personal life.
- You know what is important to you.
- You know how you want both your personal and your business life to be.
- You have confidence about your ideas.
- You are so clear about what you want that asking for it becomes a cinch.
- Your business and your personal life work in alignment with one another.
- You know where you are going.
- You wake up each morning full of energy, knowing exactly what you want to achieve that day.
- You are fired up about your current life and your future.
- You are excited about what you do.
- You find making decisions a no-brainer.
- You easily recognize opportunities when they show up.
- You no longer procrastinate.
- You know long-term exactly what you want out of life.
- You are so crystal clear about what you want that other people find it easy to give you what you need.

But if you really looked at it, the simplicity of goal setting really is: look at where you are today; identify where you want to be tomorrow, and create a plan of action to take you there.

FAMILY GOALS

It is worthwhile to sit down with your children and teach them how to set goals. They need to go through the exact same process that we have just discussed. The earlier a person learns to set goals, the more natural it will be for them as they get older. By doing this they will also begin to see how the process works and will learn to be over-achievers. Educating your children on how to set their personal goals and establishing family goals should be considered quality time well spent.

I started the process of sitting down with my son to set goals when he was fifteen. I recommend you start much earlier, maybe when your children are eight or nine. I gave him the pitch of how important it is and how effective it can be to help him get to where he wants to be. He was okay with that part. It was when I said we had to write them down in detail and put time frames around them that I got, "Dad I am not doing that, it's stupid. Give me break." Okay, so I needed to do a little more work here. You would think I was speaking a foreign language to him since he obviously didn't understand me. When I pulled out my goal plans and showed him my plans from years past as well as the current year's plan, he seemed to understand English again. I explained and showed him how much this has helped me to achieve certain things in my life. After that he reluctantly agreed to get some paper and a pencil.

We started with his football goals for the upcoming season. Like all goal-planning, the detail is critical. We wrote down how much he wanted to weigh, how much he wanted to bench press, what he wanted his forty-yard-dash time to be. He continued his list into the season itself: what he wanted his yards-per-carry to be, his total yards, number of touchdowns and total pass receptions. Then we moved from football to educational goals. This information didn't flow quite as swiftly, but he finally came up with it:

what he wanted his G.P.A. to be and what he would do to ensure he would accomplish it. We went through family goals and the other items on the list that were applicable. It is important to keep in mind these were *his* goals. My role was to help facilitate the process and teach him how to goal-plan. The process falls short if it is you who sets the goals for someone else to achieve. If you find that to be the case, you need to kick yourself off the bus.

To my delight, at the end of the season when we reviewed the list of goals he'd written before the season began, he had achieved 95 percent of them. Of course I immediately took this opportunity to remind him of the value of goal-setting. From this point on, he was on automatic pilot. Every year I asked him if he had written his goals, and he always said, "yep," or that he was in the process.

Football was an excellent vehicle to teach Robbie the value of goal planning. Everyone needs to set goals with a burning desire toward achieving them. I hope my son and everyone else reading this sets their goals and writes them down *every* year. If you want this process to work for you, it is important to be consistent. Goals put you on the highway to being successful!

CHAPTER FOUR

KNOWING THE PLAYBOOK

KNOWLEDGE

Football is a game played with arms and legs and shoulders,
but mainly from the neck up.

KNUTE ROCKNE

Football players learn early on that they always have to be increasing their knowledge to stay competitive on the field. Football offers a great opportunity to learn many of life's lessons in a controlled environment.

Knowledge as I understand it includes a complete understanding of experiences, facts, ideas, and insights a person acquires during their lifetime. I'm not just talking about formal schooling. That's only one type of classroom. Truth is, everyone's life is a 24/7 classroom. When you know the different processes and ways to acquire knowledge, you'll be able to win any game you decide to play.

This chapter takes a look at these processes and ways you can acquire knowledge, both on and off the playing field.

LEARNING FROM PENALTIES

Every football player who ever played the game has made mistakes, missed assignments, broken a rule, and paid a price for it. In every football game, inevitably, someone on the offensive team jumps offside. The casual observer might wonder if the offending player is a moron or what? How hard it is to remember what the snap count is when you were just told three seconds before? The penalty is only five yards. The player is embarrassed. He usually gets an earful from the coach; he also gets to "ride the pine" while he thinks about improving his concentration and listening skills. This sounds terrible, especially if it costs the team a first down or worse. There are no real mistakes in football, just lessons learned. And if the worst lesson you learn results in a five-yard or (heaven forbid) a fifteen-yard penalty, you'll have live a charmed life.

Out in the real world, if you are driving and not concentrating on what you are doing, the consequences are severe. If you suddenly run a red light, the penalty for that can be *your life*. If you drive around drinking and get into an accident, that penalty can cost you fifteen years in jail, not just fifteen yards. Instead of the referee blowing his whistle and calling unnecessary roughness, a policeman blows his whistle and calls unnecessary ignorance. For that whistle, you spend an extended period on the sideline—in jail!

Football players acquire valuable knowledge by receiving large doses of both positive and negative reinforcement for their actions. It is the knowledge learned from these lessons that helps them navigate between the lines of life.

TOUGH-LOVE LEARNING

There is a saying that all the Beck children are familiar with (and don't really care for): "Give a man a fish and you feed him for a day. Teach a man to fish and you feed him for a lifetime." Of course we would all like everything handed to us. Nowadays it's hard for a parent to not bait their kid's hook, throw out the line, and reel in every fish their kids ask for: trust me, my kid's have been spoiled. It wasn't that way for me or my wife. We have more than our parents did. Our too-smart kids also see that we could give them even more than we already do.

"More" refers to more material things and more money. It doesn't mean more support or more life lessons and love. It's those last three things that count. But in today's material, got-to-have-it-now world, it gets easier and easier to just give kids the whole fish. Do you ever wonder how we survived as kids or young adults without cell phones, pagers, X-boxes, color TV's in our rooms, designer clothes, computers, and a host of other nice-to-haves that seem to be absolute necessities in our children's minds? Maybe this is just an updated version of the things we heard from our parents. When *they* were kids, they walked uphill both ways to school in six feet of snow with holes in their shoes. Okay, maybe that's a bit of an exaggeration. In any event, the trick as a parent is to know how and when to stop handing over the fish and start handing over the rod and reel.

Coaches can give their players guidance, but when it comes to game-time it's up to the players to get the job done. No one can do it for them. That's how the real world works too. Too many kids who never played football—or any other sport for that matter—have issues when it's time for them to stand on their own. The same is true for the football players who are unable to connect the dots and understand the true meaning and secret of football.

There are many stories where a player might have had a misguided coach who creates cakewalk opportunities for him to skate through school, just to keep him eligible. The player then graduates and finds himself unable even to read—he has no chance in life.

I saw a symptom of this firsthand when I traveled to see my son play in a game against the University of Nebraska his freshman year in college. It was the fifth game of the season. I was standing in the lobby waiting for the team to come out so we could send them off with a big cheer. While waiting, I saw the team's academic advisor. I took the opportunity to talk with her to check on my son's grades. Her reply was surprising.

She said, "Well his name hasn't shown up on any list so he must be doing okay. But Mr. Beck, you need to make sure your expectations are set correctly. You see, your son is a true freshman. He's busy playing. He travels weekly and he has a demanding class schedule in addition to his football practice time requirement. Our school also has a challenging academic curriculum."

I said that I understood all that. Then I asked where my expectations should be. She replied, "If your son achieves a 1.67 grade point average for his first semester, you should be happy."

I thought, *"1.67? You must be joking! That's barely eligible!"* The players had mandatory study hall if their grades were below a 2.0, so I knew the school subscribed to teaching men how to fish versus feeding them for a day. However, the expectation level was so low, how could they be expected to succeed after college?

My grade point expectations had always been high for my son. Fortunately, that was the standard he adopted for himself. The result? He got a 3.0 GPA his first semester and maintained it for four years.

On the flipside, one of my best friends in college who came from a very comfortable family never really got the chance to understand how the real world works. He had a swanky high-rise apartment near campus, a new car, credit cards, and a weekly stipend of money sent to him. His nickname was "Prince." He never played football.

Prince took seven years to obtain his four-year undergraduate degree. The last I heard, he was still getting money regularly from his dad. By the way, his dad's nickname was "King."

LEARNING BY DOING

There are some people like Prince who just keep attending school and never graduate. They are referred to as "professional students." Their philosophy or code of life is "knowledge is power." I don't totally agree with that. Knowledge by itself has limited use unless it is applied. Just sitting in a classroom environment and memorizing lots of data does not provide much unless one can apply that knowledge to a plan of action.

Industrialist Charles Kettering said, "The difference between intelligence and education is that intelligence applied will make you a good living." That viewpoint is pretty difficult to debate. Applying knowledge learned in the classroom or on the football field to the real world is one of the keys to evolving as an individual.

The practical application of theoretical knowledge is the difference between fantasy and reality. It's a player's (or anyone's) experiences that contribute to their reservoir of knowledge and increases their ability to process valuable information. Transposing that information into purposeful action is the real value of acquiring knowledge. If one doesn't apply their knowledge, the best they can hope for is to be a consistent winner in the game of Trivial Pursuit. The key word here is trivial. It is a shame to waste one's life in trivial pursuits. It's putting what you learn into practical or tactical action that gives you the capability of dealing with life's ever-changing and demanding circumstances.

VALIDATE YOUR GUT FEELINGS

Have you wondered why a player suddenly zigs instead of zags? How at the very last minute, the receiver turns around and catches the ball? Some folks call it their "gut feeling." Others call it "common sense." Whatever you call it, it's the ability to acquire knowledge without a tangible reasoning process—a feeling that you are certain you're right, even if you cannot explain why. Some call it an educated guess.

Depending on your "gut feeling" as a success strategy is not very prudent, especially today with so much data available all around you. By doing a little digging, you can find out anything you need to know. So why not make informed decisions? As a last recourse, however, when all other avenues have been exhausted, you can then look to your "gut feeling" to make a decision.

As you read this you might disagree with my concept about the value of gut feelings. Maybe you have done quite well following your gut feelings, wherever they come from. I'm certainly not an expert in epistemology (the study of knowledge), but I'd bet that gut feelings come from our experiences, which are available for us to draw upon.

That football player who turned around at the last split-second, just in time to catch the ball or knock the ball away, how did he know when to turn? Most likely he had an instinct to move that was based on similar experiences. The player who zigged instead of zagged may have had a negative result the last time he zagged or a positive result the last time he zigged. So he went back to what worked. Is this any different to how any of us make *our* split-second gut decisions?

Gut feelings can be useful. In business, the trick is to know how and when to verify them with research and supporting data.

A few years ago, one of my good friends whom I consult with on many business and personal matters had a vision and intuition to develop a new software product. He had years of good experience, a thorough knowledge of the marketplace, and a deep understanding of the issues his new product could solve. His gut told him to develop the product.

I call this the "build it and they will come" syndrome. A lot of business entrepreneurs fall prey to this syndrome. It's kind of like a football player reading their own press clippings and believing them. It usually is not a good idea. This time was no different. My friend learned a tough lesson, like so many do. He failed to validate his gut feeling about the product and it cost him dearly.

The data and information were available to warn him that the market didn't really exist in sufficient quantity to make his new product viable.

Unfortunately, he made a sizable investment without doing in-depth research. As a result, he wound up spending countless hours and large sums of money without producing any sales results.

Recently, in a football game there was a fourth-and-one situation. The team was inside the opponent's territory, so it was a tough call whether to go for it or punt. After a short deliberation the coach decided to go for it. The fans were delighted with this decision. They all got to their feet and cheered mightily. The hand-off went up the middle for no gain. The fans were dismayed as the ball was turned over on downs to the other team.

Later on in the same game, the team was ahead 20 – 8. It was late in the fourth quarter with the ball on the opponent's two-yard line. It was fourth down and the team needed one yard for a first down and two yards for a touchdown. What would your call be? Traditional football wisdom might say to go for it. But if you kick a field goal the team goes ahead 23 – 7, forcing the opposing team to score twice. Timeout was called—probably to validate what the coach's gut feeling was telling him to do. He decided to go for the field goal. The field-goal kicker hurried onto the field. The snap was good, but the field goal was blocked! To make matters worse, the team wound up losing the game! Of course hindsight is always twenty-twenty. It is also easy for everyone in the stands, media, and even players to say they should have gone for it. What was the coach thinking?

I'll tell you what he was thinking—about the previous fourth-and-one earlier in the game when his offense did not convert. He was also calculating—based on his past experience—that his chances were pretty good that the kicker would make a twelve-yard field goal and that this would put his team ahead by two scores. Even though the result was not the desired one, the coach still made the right decision based on his experience.

The "school of hard knocks" is the source of valuable and useful knowledge and training. Business giants like Ray Kroc, the founder of McDonalds, and Walt Disney didn't have formal business educations. One day, when I was in college, I was speaking to a successful older gentleman. I was frustrated about a concept in one of my courses that didn't seem relevant. He told me not to worry too much about it. He then said that it had been forty years since he had graduated from college. "How much do you think what I learned in college is still applicable today?" That really made me stop and think. It made perfect sense; you gain experience and knowledge from the situations and problems of day-to-day living.

Football players literally bump into those hard knocks everyday on the field. They start early in peewee football. If they are not focused and aware of what is going on around them, they can have painful learning experiences. As they pick themselves up off the ground, you see them register their hard-won knowledge of life. Football gives players lots of opportunities to learn the hard way. Granted, out in the world, there aren't always huge paychecks or fame. No one gets a fancy degree or officially graduates from the School of Hard Knocks. Still, we are all life-long students in this institution and attendance *is* mandatory.

BECOME A LIFELONG LEARNER!

Abraham Lincoln said "I don't think much of a man who is not wiser today than he was yesterday." I couldn't agree more.

None of us should be content with the knowledge we have. Everyone—whether you are a professional athlete, career professional, parent, or teacher—needs to continue the learning process in order to improve. The most successful managers I work with, regardless of their position in the company or knowledge base, are willing to learn.

Egos are probably the number one reason why entrepreneurs and senior mangers fail. Weak leaders become defensive when people try to help by offering them knowledge. Strong leaders never let their egos get in the way of their learning or decision-making processes.

I was once consulting with a company, helping them improve their revenue growth. Their revenues were about $500 million in sales. They had been in business for a number of years. They wanted to increase their market share and make some changes. I put their organization through extensive assessment processes identifying issues that might be impeding their growth. Sometimes the outcome of such assessments is not fun when I have to relay the results to the senior management.

On this particular assignment, there were a considerable number of changes that needed to be implemented. One critical step I had not had the chance to execute was an interview/ interface with the CEO/ President.

Many large companies like this one are run by executives who are so intimidating that people are not comfortable or capable of interfacing with them. Everyone does their best to avoid them. However, real organizational change typically comes from the top down. So to effectively impact and influence change in this organization, I felt the need to meet and discuss issues and attitudes with the CEO.

When I brought this up to the Executive Vice President I had been working with, he was visibly uncomfortable. After a lot of selling and a reasonable explanation why this meeting would be in his best interest, he agreed to try to set up a meeting. He timidly asked if "his master" would meet with me.

The Executive VP was surprised when he returned with the news, "Jack will see you now, but for just a few minutes." Wow! I felt almost privileged that the

CEO was actually going to grant me time to help him. I walked into his office, which was the size of a small apartment. It had all the trappings of massive success. It was on the top floor, heavy wood paneling, sectional leather couch, a bar—all the comforts one would expect for a person in that position.

He welcomed me and told me to take a seat. My first question was, "Do you know what I have been doing here for the last several weeks?" His reply was, "Oh sure. You have some unique way of evaluating our people."

I quickly told him I wasn't doing anything like that. Now I really had his attention. I told him I had been gathering information from all the departments about the issues the company was experiencing. I told him that in two weeks I would be back with a detailed report explaining these issues and my opinions as to why they existed. I also said in a nice way that he was probably going to get his feelings hurt and if he didn't want to hear the findings there was no sense in my going through the exercise.

He laughed a little and said, "You aren't going to beat me up, are you?" (I was quite a bit physically larger than this guy). I answered, "No, but you might have to spend some time in my woodshed for some of the things that are going on here." He loved that I had the gall to say that and I ended up not leaving his office for two hours!

This CEO of a $500 million-dollar company shared with me that his expertise was not in sales. It was in logistics management. He welcomed my advice, and was very teachable. This CEO was a life-long learner. Consequently, he was a successful manager and a good leader. He made the recommended adjustments and changes and was able to achieve the revenue results the organization was looking for.

There is an opportunity to learn something from every person you meet and in every situation you find yourself. Everyone has had a host of unique and special experiences. It doesn't matter what the person's position in life is, how successful, or unsuccessful they are, how old or how young they are.

In fact, we can learn a lot from our children. My kids teach me things all the time. My daughter Melissa has an unshakable outgoing and pleasant personality. She talks to everyone, at any time, in any circumstance, and doesn't have the shyness bone that holds so many people back. It is so impressive to watch her work a room with ease, getting people to adore her almost as much as I do. I am not introverted by any stretch of the imagination, but I learn from watching how her sincere interest in other people ends up making her fast friends.

Our baby boy Nick (who is nineteen) is very laidback and unassuming, without a worry in the world. He genuinely enjoys life and has fun. Most of us sometimes forget about having fun and being laidback. The everyday pressures and responsibilities tend to weigh on all of us from time to time. Nick just seems to have the words written on his face everyday, "Don't worry. Be happy."

Tyler our third-oldest child is pursuing a career in medicine. I learn from his sincere passion to want to help people every time I speak with him. He is noble in his quest and is pursuing his career choices for all the right reasons. We would all be better individuals by taking a page out of Tyler's book.

My lovely wife teaches me, too. She teaches me how to love, how to give back, and what's important in life. Without her and the kids, on some days there would be no obvious reason to get out of bed in the morning.

You should make it a daily goal to learn something from every person you meet.

Embrace Change
as a Learning Opportunity

Going on a quest for knowledge and making it a lifelong commitment lubricates the internal gears that enable you to be able to change. In football, every day, every week, every game is different. At the professional level of football you might even play for a different team from one week to the next. Players have to be able to adopt changes, learn from the change, and be open to new ways to do things.

It's the same in every business, including yours.

One of my favorite questions from the course my company Sales Builders offers is, "Do you think the world we live in has changed recently?" Everyone ponders this question for a few seconds and says, "Yes." Then I ask, "How?" Everyone is quick to offer all the ways our current environment has been impacted by 9/11 or the current economic conditions.

The next question: "Do you think the way business is done over the last few years has changed?" Again, after an even briefer pause, they all say, "yes." We then have a lively discussion where everyone participates and gives his or her opinion about how the world has changed, how business has changed, and how it has affected them.

The final question is, "Since you all agree the world we live in has changed and how we do business has changed, what have *you* changed about your sales approach?" The room suddenly gets as quiet as that moment after the visiting team scores a winning touchdown as the clock runs out.

Learning means change. When you acquire knowledge you develop, grow and ultimately change and evolve. This is hard for people who are uncomfortable with unfamiliar situations that challenge their normal way of thinking and acting.

Getting people to learn and accept the changes they need to make is by far the toughest part of training a group of sales professionals. It's not easy recognizing the fact that you're missing steps, that you haven't been asking the right questions, that you've been selling to the wrong person, or that you've been selling the same way you did four years before.

When you embrace change as a learning opportunity, you'll be able to reprogram misconceived notions you learned over the years. Too many people allow change to paralyze them as though they had some incurable disease. This will, without question, restrict your personal growth (and your bank account.) The only thing that is consistent is change. Anticipate it. Welcome it. And learn from the experiences change will offer you. Seek it out—wherever you are, and from whomever you're with.

One of the best ways I learn is from interaction with others in a group setting. Every group offers a variety of knowledge and experience that I learn from. Group learning is effective when problem-solving or brainstorming is the goal.

Brainstorming is a group of individuals throwing out random thoughts with the goal of developing a new idea or resolving a situation or problem. Having the right group can offer insight and knowledge you might not have. The trick is to always be sure you get the right group together.

Returning to my friend who tried to develop a new software package, I discovered he conducted some level of brainstorming and group learning as he was developing his product. The mistake he made was not getting the right group of people. They either had less knowledge than he did or they were too nice to tell him there was not a market for his product.

The key is to also keep an open mind. I've been involved in countless situations where I was brought in to help validate a thought or an idea. What the management team really wanted was a yes-man. I am the wrong person to bring in if you don't want an honest appraisal of your current idea or situation. There is little benefit in giving bad information just to make someone feel good. This applies to sports, business, friends, and even family. If my kids do something good, I love offering praise. I look for as many ways to praise them as I can. The other side of the coin holds true as well. When they make a mistake, get outside the lines, or screw up in some way, they need to hear about that as well so they can learn from it. I'm not helping if I am praising mistakes or mediocre efforts.

The real world does not work that way. The faster they understand that, the better off they will be. No one has the need or the use for a yes-man who just agrees with the group and offers little value or original thought. Remember, try not to take a controlling position in group-learning situations. We all have a tendency to fall in love with our ideas and visions. Keep an open mind. This concept is reinforced regularly in football by the teamwork aspects of the game.

HAPPY EARS

One must be careful not to influence the group too much to come around to your way of thinking or you dilute the process. You will not receive benefit from the group experience if you do. Also guard against what I call "happy ears." Happy ears are when you hear just what you want to hear and filter out the rest. It can also be called selective hearing.

Many of us tend to hear only what we want to hear in order to validate our thoughts or position on a subject. As such, we just tune out anything that goes against our position. Every once in a while my wife will develop a case of selective hearing. However, to stay out of the doghouse, I think I'll leave those stories in my head and relate a case of happy ears about my son instead.

I made a deal with my kids that if they received a full scholarship to college, I would buy them a car. Considering the price of the average college education today, that was a win-win situation for them and for me.

When Robbie received a full five-year athletic scholarship to one of the best universities in the country, I was happily on the hook for a car. One day after his freshmen year, he come up to me and said, "Hey Dad, if I make the all-conference team, will you buy me a Cadillac Escalade?" Keep in mind, a Cadillac Escalade was a nicer car than I drove or the car my wife drove. (She also gets the best car—I'm not stupid.)

After picking myself up off the floor from laughing, I asked him if he was serious. He then proceeded to give me a fairly weak sales pitch as to why his request was reasonable (he has improved his selling skills considerably since then). He let me know how much money he'd saved me by earning a scholarship to college. Also, since I had promised to buy him a car, what was the big deal? That's all my kids' favorite question. "What's the big deal?"

He went on to tell me that if he made all-conference, it would help his quest to be drafted into the NFL. This was an extreme case of selective hearing, Happy Ears. The first thing I had to do was pull out my virtual parenting handbook and look for the section on college education.

As I flipped through the virtual pages, I couldn't seem to find where it said a parent had to pay for their kids' college education. Amazingly, this information came as somewhat of a surprise to him. That was the first blow to his pitch for a new Escalade.

The next awakening was when I asked him how his making all-conference benefited me. He stumbled for a second, and then came out with something like, "You'll be proud of me for achieving that." I was already extremely proud of him, so that argument fell short too. Lastly, and most importantly, I reminded him: "I said I would buy you a car, not a life-style!"

The moral of the story was that he did not get his Cadillac Escalade. The poor boy had to settle for a Ford Sportrac. Please don't turn me into child services.

GET OUT OF THE BOX

Another important concept in the quest for knowledge is applying "out of the box thinking." Out of the box thinking is daring to be different, not conforming to the norm, and challenging conventional wisdom.

We all need to get out of our comfort zone if we are to continue to evolve. You have to be willing to be an independent thinker. Independent thinking is reaching decisions or making judgments based on your own experiences, beliefs, and observations. The alternative is to simply rely on the opinions of others.

"Out of the box thinking" involves being a non-conformist and not falling prey to what others believe. Sometimes you have to think outside the box and be willing to go it alone. Kick returners and punt returners all understand out-of-the-box-thinking. There are a lot of times a play is set up to the right, with a wall of blockers lined up to pave the way for a long runback. After a couple of steps to the right, the returner cannot see a wall. The only thing he does see is a group of angry headhunters wanting to make him a permanent part of the stadium. Suddenly he changes directions. At this point he is basically on his own. The coach has called for a return-right. The returner observes that the plan has broken down, so he goes return-middle in the hopes of making a big play on his own.

If we just line up with everyone else's thoughts and ideas or if we wait for someone else to tell us what to do, the very best we will ever be is average.

When you are average, you are just as close to the bottom as you are to the top. Put me in a pine box and send me on a slow train back to Georgia before I become average! Average people compare themselves to other people. Exceptional achievers compare and hold themselves accountable to their full potential.

Develop an independent frame of mind. In other words don't let others create for you a destiny and vision you don't see or believe in. I sometimes refer to this as an entrepreneurial spirit.

A good example is my close friend George. He got out of college and took a job selling computer hardware. George had played football for years. He understood the principle secrets of the game of football, so he had that advantage. However, all George knew about computer hardware was that he knew absolutely nothing about it.

What George also knew was that—at that time—the average income for a college graduate was about $15,000. Most importantly, George knew that the sales people who made their numbers in his company earned over $100,000!

This company had an interesting training program for the newbees. You were sent to Silicon Valley in California for a few months. The first two weeks, you were put in an orientation class to learn about the company and what you were about to sell. When the limo at the San Francisco airport picked up George and his dry-cleaning bag (he didn't even have a suitcase), all he could think about was that they would soon see through him and back he would go. What had he gotten into?

The new sales people had the lucky task of selling the used equipment the company took in trade when a new system was sold. After that they threw you in the deep end pretty quickly. You either succeeded and got a territory, or they sent you back on the next plane.

At the time there were four new trainees trying to sell the used equipment. The other guys had been there a couple of weeks already so they were already banging away on the phones. Incidentally, none of them were ex-football players like George. He joined these guys who were already in a bullpen (a group of cubicles in an open part of the office), each armed with a phone and a list of names to call.

These lists were tattered and full of names who'd been called dozens of times by every other group of new salespeople who'd come to the company since its inception. Every night, these guys would come back to the shared apartment, beaten down because of the lack of success. George's time in the bullpen was coming up soon. He just couldn't face being sent back as a failure and settling for a mediocre job. He had to apply out-of-the-box-thinking just to survive.

He knew that he had to figure out some creative strategy other than calling the same people everyone else had called, hoping to find a needle in a haystack. He thought back to the creativity he'd learned and applied when playing football. Finally he found some daylight; he would go to the accounting department and ask for a list of all the customers who had previously bought used equipment from the company.

The following day, Accounting delivered a handsome, crisp new list of names to call. Of course, George hadn't asked anyone for permission to implement his strategy. He was afraid they would make him conform to what everyone else was doing.

With his list in hand and his plan of action set, George starting calling clients. He called the customers and told them the company had an overstock of used equipment, which was true. He then said that since they were a preferred customer, he wanted to offer them the first chance to buy. To George's delight, the plan worked better than he could have imagined! George single-handedly sold the entire inventory. For his efforts he received $10,000, won a car, and got the pick of the litter of territories!

Whether you succeed or fail, independent thinking is usually rewarded. People are more likely to evolve when they are willing and able to initiate action independently without direction from some controlling authority above them. The more independent your thinking is, the more likely your confidence will grow. Results that come from your independence make it easier and easier to face whatever fears hold you back. Football is an excellent training ground here as well.

Freshmen are almost always very timid and shy when they show up at summer camp. They want to make a good impression on the coaches and the other players. It is very rare for a freshman to come into camp thinking outside the lines. As they get more comfortable with the coaches, the other players, and their own abilities, they begin to test the lines. It's usually a good idea to initially stay reasonably inside the lines and do what's wanted and needed. Once you've done that, it's certainly okay to ride right up on the lines. It's only out of bounds if you step over the line too soon.

Knowing when the time is right to cross that (and any) line depends on how you respond to any given situation. As I see it, there are basically four ways available for you to respond. From my perspective, there are four categories of people in the world. We all fit in to one of these categories that I describe in the next few pages.

1. THE UNCONSCIOUS COMPETENT

An Unconscious Competent is a person who intuitively does the right things but isn't sure how. They are not aware of, nor do they have, a repeatable and measurable routine or pattern. They just seem to be at the right place at the right time. When asked what they do differently than everyone else, they aren't sure. These people can be productive, but they do not make very good leaders. To be an effective leader, you have to be able to transfer your skills and teach others to apply your approach to success.

An example of this might be when you ask someone for directions. How many times have you heard, "I know how to get there, but I can't explain it to you exactly." If that person can easily arrive at the destination you are seeking, but can't communicate the route to you, it is a good bet that they are an Unconscious Competent.

2. THE UNCONSCIOUS INCOMPETENT

An Unconscious Incompetent is a person who is completely lost and has no direction. They don't know if they are succeeding or if they are missing opportunities. They find it difficult to get wherever they are going, much less trying to explain the route to anyone else. They struggle in all areas of life.

3. THE CONSCIOUS INCOMPETENT

A Conscious Incompetent is one who knows exactly where they want to go, they just don't know how to get there. They are not sure how to acquire the means or skills to reach the destination they have set their sights on. They are at least on the right track. If they have the conviction necessary, they have a good chance of reaching their destination.

4. THE CONSCIOUS COMPETENT

A Conscious Competent knows where they are going and knows how to get there. These people understand the secret of football. They are applying the important attributes of success and have made them part of their core being. If you ask them for directions, they will tell you in an understandable fashion. They will also draw a detailed map, complete with street names, landmarks, and tell you the number of stop signs and traffic lights along the way. It is rare to find a conscious competent person who does not apply most of the attributes of success we discuss in this book.

Which category would you place yourself in? It's okay if you are not a Conscious Competent right now. If you apply the concepts contained in this book, you will move into this category. You might arrive as a Conscious Competent sooner than you think.

What category do you think the typical football player falls into when they are playing the game? My assessment is that most players start out in the Unconscious Competent category. They have the skills, the speed, and the strength to play the game. Through hard work and coaching they quickly move into the Conscious Competent category. If they don't move into this category, they won't be able to execute the plays, survive on the field, or get much playing time.

An Unconscious Incompetent player has to move extremely quickly out of this category or they will get hurt. In fact it's rare to see this type of individual take up football for very long. In the game of football, players can't walk around with their heads in the clouds. If a player, barely getting by, is going through the drills, not paying attention, there are enough Conscious Competent players around who will take advantage of them.

If a person is an Unconscious Incompetent in the game of life, they are leaving themselves open to being taken advantage of as well. It's a tough category to live in. They might know what they want, but they might not have the skills to achieve it. Either they acquire the skills needed or they are forced to adjust to the unsatisfying destination. Some in this category can move up by applying the attributes of success contained in this book.

Conscious Competent players are what every coach wants and what every player strives to be. Show me a team full of Conscious Competent players and I'll show you a championship team.

Every one of us needs to strive to be a Conscious Competent. Football, in its unique way, helps players achieve this category. It is up to the player to make the needed adjustments, to fill those gaps that stand between him and the category of Conscious Competent. If they do, they will move to greater things on and off the field. If they can't, or they aren't willing to do the necessary work, they won't move forward.

COLLABORATION

Another important kind of interaction is the ability to collaborate. This happens when two people with a different set of skills or knowledge each takes responsibility for the success of the other person. On the football field an offensive tackle blocks for a running back. They both depend on each other to succeed. If the offensive tackle doesn't make his block, the running back is likely to get tackled. If the running back doesn't "find the hole" freed up by the block, the play will go nowhere. An offensive coach and a defensive coach have different knowledge but each needs to help the other if they are going to win the game.

You have to be willing to learn from bad examples and past experiences as well. If the offensive tackle goes the wrong way and is executing the wrong play, the running back might be foolish enough to blindly follow him. In a reciprocal learning situation, compromise can be dangerous. When you have compromised, there is usually a lack of accountability. You must choose to go one way or the other. The running back either blindly follows his blocker (even though he went the wrong way) or he runs the play as it was designed.

ARE YOU A LIFELONG LEARNER?

Measure your commitment to gain more knowledge by answering these ten questions.

1. When was the last book you read on your profession?

2. What have you done recently to increase your market knowledge?

3. When was the last seminar or conference you attended to increase your awareness on any given subject?

4. How many new network contacts have you made that might possess knowledge or information you might be able to learn from?

5. Do you consider your basic knowledge of your profession: consistently exceeds the average, is average, is below average, or are you an expert?

6. When was the last time you applied some out-of-the-box thinking?

7. What is the most creative thing you've done lately?

8. When was the last time you learned something new? (No fair counting what you are learning from this book, even though you *are* on the right track!)

9. How long has it been since you learned something from another's bad example?

10. Are you applying what you are learning and making changes in your behavior regularly?

If you honestly answered yes to all of these questions, then you are consistently striving to gain knowledge. Good for you! You are doing the right things. If you identified any gaps in your dedication to acquiring additional knowledge, that's good too. Now you know what you have to do to improve—and that means that you have just learned something new!

CHAPTER FIVE

BRINGING YOUR
A-GAME

ATTITUDE

Yesterday is a canceled check, today is cash on line,

tomorrow is a promissory note.

COACH HANK STRAM, NFL WINNING SUPERBOWL COACH

In the game of football, just as in life, the level of success you achieve starts with your attitude. I have never talked to a player, regardless of how much of an underdog they were going into any given game, who didn't feel they were going to win.

Recently, Appalachian State beat the powerhouse football team, Michigan Wolverines. Some are calling that one of the biggest upsets in sports history. I guarantee you if you pulled the Appalachian State players aside before the game and asked them what the outcome was going to be, they would have displayed an attitude of conviction they were going to win the game. Think about the people you know who succeed constantly in their lives. Think of the happiest, most fulfilled people you know. What is their typical attitude about life?

THREE KINDS OF PEOPLE

There are three kinds of people on life's port. People either

1. Recognize his or her ship when it comes in.

2. Don't recognize their ship when it comes in.

3. Don't wait for the ship to come in. Instead they swim out and find it.

The third type of person is the take-charge individual who is not willing to let fate dictate their level of success. Success does not happen by accident to anyone.

Opportunities don't travel on any schedule; you just have to watch for them. We sometimes wish we could be sacked out in front of the TV or playing video games all day, and out of nowhere, Mr. Success comes knocking on our door to take care of all of our needs for the rest of our lives. Wouldn't that be nice? Get off the couch! No one is coming along to knock on the door. Success happens because people create situations or circumstances that enable them to succeed.

If you think you'll be successful and happy then you likely will be so, as long as you act on your thoughts. Thinking about it alone is only the first step. On the other hand, if you have convinced yourself you won't be successful or happy, regardless of the actions you take, you will probably fail and be miserable. The only thing you can truly control in your life is your thoughts. Everything starts with a thought. If you think you can, you will. If you think you can't, you won't. Either way you're right!

Football players learn early on *can't* is not an acceptable word or thought for them. The sooner a person eliminates *can't* (and other phrases like "I don't know how," "it's too hard," "what if," "should of," "would of," and "maybe") from their thought process the sooner they begin to achieve their full potential.

People ask me how I do this. First, recognize that the only thing we can count on in our lives is change. Pat Croce (owner of the NBA Philadelphia 76ers) summed it up when he said, "No one ever stays the same. You're either getting better or you're getting worse. But simply knowing and accepting this gives you the opportunity to make your changes positive ones." And positive change starts with positive thinking.

Have you ever seen a football team run the exact same play four downs in a row when it didn't work the first time, the second time, or the third time? Most of the time there will never even be a second time. Have you ever seen a football game where in the first half of the game the one team dominated the other and was ahead by twenty or more points at halftime, then in the second half the dominated team comes back to win the game? What do you think happened in the locker room at halftime? There was change. There were attitude adjustments. There was a lot of soul searching that went on and the result was positive thinking, which changed the outcome.

It is a priceless gift for young people to understand they can be way down in a situation and turn it around regardless how hopeless it appears by making some adjustments in their attitude and actions.

Just like so many other things, having a positive outlook is not always natural. There are two basic things that have to take place to develop a positive mental attitude.

1. Get rid of negative-thinking patterns and actions

2. Develop good positive-thinking habits

Stop thinking negative thoughts. Sounds easy enough. Here's how: Recognize when you have one and replace it with a positive thought.

My ninty-six-year-old grandmother was sitting around one day listening to my wife and I talking about the South Beach diet, the Zone diet, the Akins diet and she got sick of listening to us and came out with some profound words. She said, "In my day the best diet was just shut your mouth and quit putting too much food in it." It's pretty hard to disagree with that logic. Okay, I know it is easy to say and much harder to do, just like it is hard to quit thinking negative thoughts. So, I'll help you get started by giving you a list of things that should help.

20 Steps to Get Rid of Negative Thinking:

1. Identify the negative people who throw you negative thoughts. If you catch these thoughts, throw them away. (Don't throw them back.)

2. Minimize your contact with these people.

3. Write down every negative word or phrase you say or think.

4. Replace it with a positive thought.

5. Develop a plan with your positive thoughts that you put into action to change your situation.

6. Keep a daily journal for one week, writing down what is or was so bad about your day. You will likely see a pattern develop over time, making it easier for you to determine who or what is making you negative.

7. In your journal, also write one good thing you did for yourself, one good thing someone did for you, one good thing you saw another do for themself, and one good thing you saw others do for others.

8. Be consistent with all the above actions.

9. Surround yourself with positive people you'd like to emulate.

10. Build on your strengths.

11. Determine what would make you happy, thus more positive.

12. Create a step-by-step action plan with dates associated with each action.

13. Pick a person or a group of people you can help to make happy. If you are ever feeling sorry for yourself go to a shelter and volunteer. For that matter, volunteer anyway to help anyone less fortunate. It will make you feel good and make their life better.

14. Everyday, for one month, make a list twenty-five positive words and phrases you can think of. Write them down. Just thinking about these words won't do the trick.

15. Post this list of words somewhere so you will see it many times a day. It will soon come natural for you to incorporate these words and phrases into your daily conversations and thought processes.

16. Be purposeful in your quest for a positive mental attitude.

17. Be decisive and don't look backwards. Hesitation will bring back negative thoughts like "what if," "should of," "would of," "could of," "maybe," and "can't."

18. Again, be consistent.

19. Practice. Practice. Practice doing this list.

20. Practice some more.

You probably didn't build negative thought patterns overnight, and it might take a little time to weed them out. If we revert back to our diet analogy for a second—most of us took a number of months at least, and maybe years, to put on that unwanted ten to fifteen pounds. You can't just diet for a week and think that weight is suddenly going to fall off. Your thought process works in the same way. The second stage to any weight loss program is that you have to maintain the weight once you have lost those pounds. If you work to lose the weight and then go back to eating the exact same way you did before, guess what happens? Thinking positive works the same way. It is a conscious life-style change. Again, not unlike a diet, every once in awhile you can indulge yourself with a treat and not blow up over night.

The same is true with the way we think. You will find once you are aware of your negative thoughts and you have the strategies readily available for how to get rid of them, your confidence will also grow. The more your confidence grows, the more positive you'll become.

LEMONS TO LEMONADE

Internalize the belief that every time something bad happens, something good will come out of it *if you look for the positive aspect.* You may not be able to recognize it at the time and many people seldom actually take the time to reconcile the good things that happen as a result of bad events.

Football players lose games all the time. Football players make mistakes in every game they play. Some mistakes cause injury and pain that a player does not soon forget. Even the peewee players can learn to turn these bitter mistakes and losses into sweet success. Each mistake offers an opportunity to learn something from it. All sports offer these life lessons. Football is just sometimes a little harsher in reinforcing it. Just remember: from lemons come lemonade.

Next time something positive happens to you, I'll bet the foundation of it, if you trace it all the way back, started with something negative. Take my challenge on this and you'll be amazed how it works. I've done this exercise myself and I've been able to trace my positive outcomes to a negative beginning almost every time. Once you understand and validate this concept for yourself, you will be able to handle life's curve balls.

To help you develop this ability, let's do an exercise. Write down five to ten positive situation or aspects in your life. Then tie each one back to a negative event that created the opportunity for the positive event to occur. See how many positive things came from harsh lessons?

PRACTICE 1-2-3

For most people this positive thought process does not come naturally. Just as with anything we want to change, you will have to work at it. If you practice enough and stick with it, a positive mental attitude and thought pattern will become part of your personality. There is not a set time that I can offer you about when this will suddenly kick in. It is a gradual process, but it works with practice.

Football players understand the concept of practice very well. It's not unusual for a team to practice a play over and over again until every step and every move becomes second nature to everyone involved. Too many times in the world outside of athletics people get away from practicing newly learned skills and try to take short cuts. Bad habits form too quickly when you have this approach.

There are very few things we do that don't require practice. Make the time, invest in yourself, practice these exercises, and you can change the way you process situations. Then the issues that might be holding you back in your life will go away. Regardless if you are getting ready for a football game or just going to work on Monday, you can practice to posses the right attitude and prepare mentally to succeed.

NOTHING VENTURED, NOTHING GAINED.

Rob played football for a small Division I college football program. You never knew what kind of season the team would have from year to year. They played a big time schedule and were in a very competitive conference. Every year they would play at least one team and often two or three teams that were ranked in the top ten best teams in the nation. Rob's team traveled to Norman, Oklahoma to play the number one ranked University of Oklahoma Sooners. The point spread on this game was a thirty-five point difference, favoring Oklahoma. A local reporter approached Rob and asked what he thought were the odds of winning the game. He said with no hesitation, "We are going to Oklahoma with the intention of winning. We have a great game plan, the week of practice was good, the team is focused, and we are hungry to win. There is absolutely no reason why we can't win this game."

The reporter kind of looked surprised and had a smirk on his face. People gave Rob's team about as much chance of winning this game as the canary has with the cat or the snowball has in the summer—you pick the saying you like. The point is, no one gave the team any chance to win.

I caught up with Rob to see what he really thought about the game. He was actually a little irritated by the question and gave me the exact same answer he gave the reporter. "We go into every game and believe we are going to win. If we don't, then why even bother playing the game?"

With a little more investigation I found out the coaches felt the same way. They all had comments like: "We are really going to surprise a lot people today," or "we know where their weaknesses are." Everyone on Rob's team believed the team was going to win even though they were up against the number one team in the country.

To start the game, just to make matters even worse, it was Oklahoma's homecoming and they were celebrating the 1985 team's national championship season. As Rob's team took the field a video proclaiming the Oklahoma season of greatness, was playing on the big screen in the stadium. Then Barry Switzer, Brain Bosworth, and just about the entire 1985 team formed a line for the current Oklahoma team to run through. The crowd was solid red (Oklahoma's color) and their covered horse-drawn wagon circled the field. The electricity and excitement in the stands for the home team couldn't have been more charged. Rob's team just waited patiently on the sidelines for this circus to end and the game to start.

I would like to end this story about belief and positive attitude by telling you this little school knocked off the number one ranked team in the nation on that Saturday but that's not what happened. What did happen is that the game ended and Oklahoma won, but only by a slim margin. Rob's team gave them more than they had bargained for on that day and his team's performance silenced a lot of people.

Believing or a having a positive attitude will not guarantee a win, but a negative defeatist attitude will guarantee a loss every time. Every Friday, Saturday, and Sunday you can see one football team beat another team that everyone was sure could never win. The winning team is full of young men who believe in themselves, their coaches, and their teammates. They go out with a "winning intent" and could care less what the odds might be. They just go out and execute their jobs to the best of their ability. Upsets happen every single week.

Too many times people defeat themselves before they ever get started. They feel the odds are too long, there are too many obstacles, and they create reasons why even trying would be futile. You might not always achieve your exact goal. The loftier and more far-reaching they are, the harder it is to obtain them. You might fall a little short of where you aimed, but you will be much further along than where you started. One thing you can take to the bank, if you don't try and give your best efforts, you absolutely won't succeed.

Who's Driving the Bus?

None of us ever would set out on a cross-county road trip without a destination in mind or without a road map guiding us on how to get to our destination. Too many people have a "make it up as they go" approach to life. Somewhere along the way the notion was believed and accepted that we have no control over the direction our lives take. Everyone has an internal bus. We have a lot of people we carry with us on this bus throughout our lives. Some popular passengers are dad, mom, wife or husband, grandpa, grandma, sister, brother, boss, co-workers, and a host of others. If you are allowing someone else to drive your bus, you don't have much control where the bus goes, they do. One thing is for sure, someone is always "driving the bus." The passengers are always giving you directions and telling you don't do that, go here, you can't do that, if you do that then this will happen, etc. There are a lot of people talking to you all at once with conflicting directives and advice. Some people get frustrated with their direction and just let someone else drive. They are always the followers. Since someone is going to drive the bus, it might as well be you! There's nothing wrong with listening to some of the passengers you choose to carry around on your bus, but you are making the final decision where you go and how to get there.

There also may be people you need to kick off your bus. What we think other people expect of us can be paralyzing at times. These can be people in our past and may be long gone or someone we see or talk to everyday. You definitely want to keep the positive influencers as a passenger, helping you at every turn. Pull your bus over and get rid of the passengers that are sarcastic, negative, giving you bad directions, or telling you that where you want to go isn't safe or right for you. The negative passenger's voices will disguise themselves in a concerning way telling you "Better not travel as far as you are thinking, you might run out gas. If you run out of gas then.... might happen." The supportive positive voice will tell you, "Look at the gas gauge and determine how much gas you're starting out with. I'd bet you will be able to travel at least as far as you are thinking because there will be gas stations along the way. Let's go for it!"

Stop reading for just a minute and make a list of all the passengers you are carrying around on your bus. Now separate the list into those who are always yelling at you to apply the brakes or who are giving bad, or offering restrictive directions. Travel with those who are there to give you positive guidance when you ask.

Sometimes this can be tough, especially when you're surrounded by negative influences who might be a misguided parent, or a nasty boss, or both. However, recognizing these negative passengers is half the battle. Years ago I stood on the sidelines and watched such a person violate and destroy his son's self-esteem. At the time I didn't realize how serious the damage would be.

STEVE'S NEGATIVE PASSENGER

The boy's name was Steve. He was fourteen when I knew him and was a terrific athlete. He was bigger than most of his peers, stronger, and faster too. He was the star of his JV football team, with an unlimited amount of promise.

His only problem was his dad. Steve's dad had been a star player in high school, a defender with a reputation for maniacal behavior, a guy who would run up and down the field, knocking aside anyone who got between him and the ball carrier. He was the best player in the state—at least, according to him.

But a back injury cut short his football career, and he never had a chance to play at the college level. If he had, he would've been a shoo-in for the Heismann Trophy—or at least that's the way he told the story. Isn't it amazing, all the wonderful things people could've done, provided they didn't have to do them out on the field?

The problem came when Steve took up football. It was obvious from the start that his dad was going to be one of those people who made darn sure his son accomplished all the things he never had, no matter the cost. He would have his glory through his boy, because that would somehow prove that he'd have done the same thing, if only....

So he pushed Steve mercilessly. Now, there's nothing wrong with pushing a player a bit. Sometimes they need that. They can be lazy, and a little nudge often can help them do what they really want to do themselves.

But what Steve's dad never learned was, it wasn't about him, it was about his son. He never discovered where the line is drawn between encouraging someone to test their limits and asking too much of a child. He didn't grasp the importance of offering lots of praise for a job well done, as well as being supportive through the inevitable setbacks.

Instead, Steve's dad put his son through impossibly long workouts in the weight room and ran the kid to death with forty-yard dashes, timing him all the while. Worst of all, nothing Steve did was good enough for his dad. It was always, "No, you have to be better, better." In truth, nothing short of Steve being the best player in the state would have satisfied his dad. And even that might not have been enough. He probably would have then expected Steve to win the Heismann Trophy and then become the highest paid player in the NFL.

The critical moment in their relationship came in eighth grade. Steve was playing in a game and, after he took an awkward hit, he fumbled the ball at a very inopportune time. The other team recovered and went on to win a close game.

Steve's dad was furious. In order to teach his son a "valuable" lesson about taking care of the ball, he made Steve carry a football under his arm, everywhere he went. For six months! I'd see Steve on the street, at the mall, in the gym, and he always had that ball.

It was silly and, worse, it was humiliating. Imagine what the other kids were saying behind Steve's back. I'm sure he could hear them, too.

Humiliation is not the right way to teach (or learn) the inner game of football. Or anything else, for that matter. It's not only wrong, it's self-defeating, which was exactly the case with Steve. Where before he'd been a great kid, solid student, fine athlete, now he started to have discipline problems, and make poor grades. One day he showed up drunk at school and threw up all over the place.

The rest is predictable. He was expelled for a while, and obviously kicked off the football team. His parents eventually had to transfer him to another school district, where I lost track of him. Maybe Steve went on to turn things around. Kids are resilient. But given who he had for a father, I doubt it.

Steve was a boy with great potential, both on and off the field, and just like that, it was gone. I'm not saying that every single thing that went wrong for Steve was due to his having to carry that football around. But I am saying that as a passenger on his son's bus, his dad criticized him constantly, yelling at him, provided no reward or recognition for his accomplishments, was not helpful. No wonder Steve crashed. His dad never gave him the chance to develop his own positive drive. He squashed Steve's self-esteem to the point where Steve's only thoughts were self-destructive.

THINK BIG

If you are going to reach for your goals, you've got be able to think positively, not destructively. Then when you are thinking positively, you've got to think big. I mean *big*! The bigger you think, the further you will travel. Big thinkers are conscious and constant goal setters. The first step is to figure out where you currently are and where you'd like to be. If we are going to embark on a trip, let's make it an adventure, a trip that will put us where we want to go.

Athletes in all sports learn to think big early. They understand the concept that you have to think big to achieve big or great things. All of my big thoughts simply came from learning the secret of football early. The most successful people don't care or encumber themselves with the reality of how things are. Instead, they visualize on how they could be, how they want them to be, and think big.

IF IT WERE EASY ANYONE COULD DO IT

No one says this is going to be easy. If it were easy, everyone would do it. All situations and opportunities present challenges; that's just part of life. Thinking positively to handle these challenges is what separates the exceptional person from the average one. You have to be willing to venture out positively and pave your own path for the pursuits you seek. If everyone did the same thing, there would never be a fast food chain that serves breakfast, suitcases with wheels, Internet, or a host of other innovations that have come along in recent years.

You *can* elevate your thinking to extend what you think you are capable of.

Ask yourself: What areas of your life can you give yourself a push in the right direction just by thinking positively—even if at this moment you're not 100 percent sure you can actually get there? Go ahead. It's a good exercise, even though it may be hard.

"Hard," by the way, is a relative term. What is hard to one person might not be hard to another. How each person evaluates the degree of difficultly is different. Sometimes things appear harder, and the obstacles are larger than they really are. It's like your mind has one of those mirrors on a car that says, things may appear larger in this mirror than they really are. Whitney Houston sings a line in one of her songs that says, "Free your mind and the rest will follow." Free your mind of negative thoughts and the negative passengers on your bus. Make a vigilant effort, and everything else will fall into place. It might not happen overnight or even in the time frame you'd like, but stick with it and it will happen.

BE INSIGHTFUL NOT IMPULSIVE

Having a vision, thinking positive, thinking big, and acting on that vision with vigilant intent and effort can be exciting—even exhilarating. But make sure you have all the required information, and do your best to support and validate your vision and plans by being insightful and not acting too impulsively.

Ron Meyer, ex head coach for the New England Patriots, commented on having nothing but excitement and emotion, "There was a lot of emotion at the Alamo and nobody survived."

ASK AND YOU WILL RECEIVE

Know what to ask, how to ask, and who to ask. This might take some research. It is a discovery process you should go through before you chart your course or change the course you are on. There are many types and different ways to ask questions that will give the most information. Make sure you are asking open-ended questions versus closed-ended questions.

An open-ended question is one that cannot be answered with a yes or a no. It forces the person to articulate their answer to you. For example: You might be networking to find contacts that will be able to offer the information you are seeking. You might be inclined to ask, "Do you know anyone that can help me with—." That is a closed ended question and the response can easily be answered no. The same question rephrased, using an open-ended technique would be, "Who do you know that could help me with—." Everybody knows someone and this question can't be answered with a yes or a no.

Write down a series of questions you might want to ask people, and make sure they are all open-ended. An example might be, "Tell be about your expectations for..." or "What did you like best about..."

Also, make sure you frame your questions with clarity, certainty, and purpose. Make sure you know what you are asking and why you are asking it. On sales calls, I have noticed sales people asking questions that, regardless of the answer the prospect offers them, will not help them move the sales cycle along or get them any closer to doing business with the company. There is no sense asking questions that lead you down the path to nowhere.

MAKE YOUR MOVE

Now you have your vision, you're thinking positive and, thinking big. You're ready to act on your vision with vigilant intent, effort, and you have all the required information. The next step is to make your move. Act decisively. Don't hesitate.

One of the things every one of us needs to evaluate when assessing risk is not just the consequences of following through, but also the cost of hesitating or of not following through. There have been more lost opportunities by people not acting on a vision than by following through and failing. If you've done the calculations, gathered the needed information, and you're willing to take action, the percentages are high that you will reach your goal.

Take this proactive approach with everything you do and you will never feel like you are a victim. The victim of circumstance mentally says, "I can't," "I won't," "It's not my fault," and all those other lame excuses you've heard.

Now is the time to stop the squabbling from your bus passengers. Choose your course, set an unhesitating, unequivocal direction whose rightness or wrongness might not be known for years. There will be challenges along the way that will test your mental abilities. These are the times when you have to really believe. If you review the past events in your life, I hope you would agree that you were able to handle the challenges you've faced. You might not have wanted to deal with certain issues. You might wish some things never occurred. But you're here now, reading this book. Oliver Wendell Holmes said, "What lies behind us and what lies before us are tiny matters compared with what lies within us." Keep that positive mental attitude and believe!

SEE WITH YOUR HEART

When Lou Little was coaching football at Georgetown, he had a player who was definitely third rate, but had so much heart he was an inspiration to the team. He rarely saw action except in the last few minutes of a game that was already decided. One day, news came that the boy's father had died. If that's not an opportunity for negative thoughts, I don't know one!

The youngster came to Coach Little and said, "Coach, I want to ask something of you that means an awful lot to me. I want to start the game against Fordham. I think that's what my father would have liked most."

Coach Little hesitated a moment, then said: "Okay, son, you'll start, but only be in there for a play or two. You aren't quite good enough and you know it."

The boy started the game and played so well, Coach Little never took him out. His play inspired the team to victory. Back in the locker room the coach embraced the young man and said, "Son, you were terrific. You never played that way before. What got into you?"

The boy answered: "Remember how my father and I used to walk around arm-in-arm? There was something about him very few people knew—he was totally blind. This afternoon was the first time my father ever saw me play."

This young man was told he was not good enough but his positive attitude helped him believe he was good enough and he was inspired by his belief that his dad was watching over him. Like that boy, if you have faith, belief, and hold that positive mental attitude, all things are possible.

CHAPTER SIX

THE GO-TO GUY

CONFIDENCE

You defeat defeatism with confidence. The man who is trained to his peak
capacity will gain confidence. Confidence is contagious,
and so is a lack of confidence.

COACH VINCE LOMBARDI

CONFIDENCE IS AN ATTITUDE

Your positive attitude is the foundation of your confidence. The most successful people and players must have a high level of confidence, which they usually earn through a series of experiences. Confidence is not just bred through success either. Of course, the more you put yourself out there, the more you try something new and succeed at it, the more you can't help but develop confidence. It begins when we are babies. We start out crawling and eventually we try walking. With every step we get better and our confidence builds until we are walking everywhere.

The same thing happens when you learn to ride a bike for the first time. Dad or mom held you while you are wobbling all over the sidewalk. You peddled away until you looked behind and dad and mom were gone. You were riding all by yourself. Your confidence grew even further. You don't need parents to help you anymore. You're a big boy now. Life is full of confidence-building experiences: going off to school for the first time, learning to drive a car, leaving home to go off to college, etc.

Don't mistake confidence for cockiness or arrogance though. Your life might be a bed of roses. You might have the "Midas Touch," turning every thing you touch into gold. You might even be the luckiest human on the planet. Congratulations, by the way if this resembles who you are. Just because everything goes your way does not mean you are better than the next person who struggles. A couple of things you can count on: things will not always go your way and you might need some help at some point in your life. Remember the story about the little mouse pulling the thorn out of the lion's paw? Everyone finds true and internal confidence attractive, but no one appreciates arrogance. Arrogance and confidence are both attitudes. They might be similar on the surface and even be members of the same family. A ferocious tiger and a Persian cat are in the same family too, but which one would you like to cuddle with and which one would you like to shoot? Let's review what some of the differences might be.

ATTRIBUTES OF CONFIDENCE

A confident person will:

- Fear their fears in an unassuming manner
- Take help from whoever will offer
- Be inspirational
- Be non-defensive
- Not be sarcastic
- Not be critical of others
- Be non-judgmental
- Not be hard-headed
- Be positive
- Have strong convictions
- Have undoubting beliefs
- Be humble
- Be strong mentally
- Find a silver lining

Arrogance is just masked insecurity. You will find that arrogant people are those who are the most unsure of themselves deep down inside. Their arrogant, unapproachable attitude is just a poorly disguised offensive approach, used as a force field. Arrogant people think they are better than everyone else because they have more money (whether they earned it themselves or not), have more material things, have an elevated position in life, and a lot of other pompous reasons. These people need to get over themselves.

ATTRIBUTES OF ARROGANCE

An arrogant person is:

- Unapproachable
- Defensive
- A know it all
- Rude
- Insecure
- Negative

- Judgmental
- Sarcastic
- Boring
- Full of themselves
- Weak
- Unpleasant

There really is a big difference in being confident versus being arrogant. Many times, people who carry themselves with a confident air are just assumed to be arrogant. That misread assumption is as wrong as mistaking a tiger for a house cat.

PERCEPTION IS REALITY

If people think you are confident then you are. If people think you are arrogant then you probably are. You might be saying you could care less what people think and say about you. You might be arrogant too. If you are going to win friends and influence people you need to care. If you are going to be an effective leader and not a dictator, you need to care. The things you do, the way you do them, along with the things you say, will create a perception about how people think and feel about you. Bo Jackson always gave interviews in the third person. Bo didn't like that... Bo does this.... Bo knows..... He was always talking about Bo as if Bo was a different person than the person who was talking. I have never met Bo Jackson so I can't say if he is arrogant or confident. I can say he came off as a very arrogant person by talking in the third person all of the time.

Creating a good perception is easy to do if you just use some common sense and think about it. It's hard to create a bad perception if you follow the age-old rule of treating people the way you would like to be treated. Consider others' feelings and getting out of the way of your shadow helps too. Arrogant people think the world revolves around them, or at least it should. They put their pants on one leg at a time too and need just as much love, nurturing, and attention as we all do. They just have a very bazaar way of expressing it. Let's test this theory about perception and reality. The following is a list of well known athletes and coaches. Just from what you have read, have seen on TV, or heard second hand, what is your perception of these people: confident or arrogant?

PERCEPTION	ARROGANT	CONFIDENT
Dion Sanders		
Dan Marino		
Mike Tyson		
Michael Irvin		
Terrell Owens		
Cal Ripken		
Barry Bonds		
John Elway		
Chris Collingworth		
Chris Carter		
Bret Favre		

Joe Montana

Dan Reeves

Bill Parcel

Al Davis

Johnny Bench

How do you think you did? Congratulations! You got 100 percent. You got them all right. I know you got them all right because perception is what they are to you. It's your impression of what you've seen, heard, and read about these athletes. Your perception is reality, so you are correct until you learn first-hand if your perception is inaccurate. Think about how you currently come across. If you could choose one person on the above list to hang out with for the day, who would it be? I'd be very surprised if it was someone you checked as arrogant.

More times than not, we root against the arrogant s.o.b.'s, whether we really know them or not. All we know is how we perceive them. Be perceived as confident and be confident. Make sure you know where the line begins and ends with arrogance.

CONFIDENCE RESERVE

Confidence is bred from trying and failing, then trying again and again until you succeed. I know you fell on your face at some point when you were learning to walk. We all did. Who never got a skinned knee from riding their bike? We got right back up and kept going until we got it right. When you failed and then conquered your set back, your confidence grew. Your confidence likely grew stronger than if you had done it right the first time without a setback. Setbacks are a part of life. The above examples of trying, failing, and succeeding built confidence in all of us. For some people when the challenges get harder, for some reason, they don't reach back in to their "confidence reserve."

Your confidence reserve is a host of successful experiences you have conquered in your life. Confidence is the gas that helps fuel your bus. However, unlike gasoline, you'll never run out of confidence. Your tank size is unlimited and you can always add more, without the first drop ever evaporating.

What happens to people between the time they learn to walk (building confidence) and the age of maturity? Why is it so hard to go and ask for that raise? Why is it so hard to make a change? Does a string of negative experiences erode confidence? Sometimes they can, but you can always revitalize your reserve.

Some people have larger reserves than others, but everyone can develop confidence. When you were little and fell off your bike, it didn't kill you, did it? It hurt, it was uncomfortable, maybe even embarrassing, but you still got right back up on that bike and rode it. Or if it was a really bad fall perhaps you waited a day. The point is, you didn't quit. You developed some degree of confidence. The younger you start filling your confidence reserve, the bigger it becomes, and the more confidence you have to draw on throughout your life.

ACCESSING YOUR CONFIDENCE RESERVE

It's indisputable that everyone has a reserve of confidence filled with positive life experiences. Even the youngest football players get this reserve filled early and often. The problem is, not everyone knows how to access their confidence reserve. And some forget they even have one. At least now, since you have read this, there is no excuse for not knowing you have a reserve you can draw on as often as you need to.

As positive situations happen, make a conscious effort to add it to your confidence reserve. Accessing your reserve is as easy as recalling a positive situation that has happened to you in the past. The fact is, you got through it and you can extract that positive experience to help you face whatever fear you might be having about a new situation.

CALL IN THE RESERVES

All sports can help to build a person's confidence reserve compartment. The game of football helps to build a young man's confidence reserve early and often in their lives. My younger son Nick was an eight-year-old who loved to play football with his brothers in the backyard. His brothers were older, bigger, faster, and stronger, but Nick liked playing with the big boys.

He would drop passes, easily get knocked down, and was generally taken advantage of by his bothers, as big bothers will do. Every time Nick went out to play in the backyard you could see his skills, determination, and confidence increase. The first time his bothers couldn't catch him, even Nick was surprised. The first time Nick tackled his twelve-year-old bother and knocked the wind out of him he knew he could not only play with the big boys, but could also hold his own. His confidence reserve grew.

Nick's confidence grew so much he wanted to sign up for Pop Warner football (our version of peewee or little league). The first time Nick put on a helmet and shoulder pads it was a little scary for him. Most of the kids had been playing with a real coach, in a structured program, with full pads for a while. Nick was also a little undersized compared to the others.

In the first practice Nick was playing defensive back and the team's running back, the best and biggest player, came around the end. Nick stuck his nose in this running back's number and got destroyed. I think the running back even stepped on his chest as he ran over him. It was not very pretty.

At this very point Nick had to make a decision, get up and do it again or walk off the field and quit. Nick figured out he didn't get killed, so he got up and went at it again. He reached back on his reserve of confidence from getting knocked around by his bothers, got up, and kept playing. That particular play was just one of the many microcosms football offers the players. This experience was just one of many that helped fill up Nick's reserve.

You have to be confident to play football at any level. If you don't have much when you start, the longer you play the fuller your confidence reserve area will be. Football as a game is a string of successes and failures, all strung together over a sixty minute period. In every game an individual player makes mistakes, has to pay for it in one way or another, and in end finds some level of success, thus building confidence.

Negative thinking erodes this confidence. This is exactly what so many people do in their lives everyday. They get started on something new and they have this tremendous, positive confidence. Everything goes well in the beginning. Whether it's a new job, a new relationship, moving to a new area, a new team—they start off with this tremendous outlook, lots of energy and passion. But after a while they grow tired. Their positive energy now turns negative, and their thoughts begin to work against them, affecting their confidence level. Questions may start, like "Did I make the right decision?" "Can I really do this?" "Maybe I should quit."

Yes, your negative thoughts create the things you might not want and depletes your confidence reserve. In the end, it is your negative, self-destructive thoughts that make it hard for you to access your confidence. We all do this, sometimes without even knowing it!

It can start when you lose your confidence and your courage while you are trying to achieve an objective. Instead of creating what you want, you start saying things like: "I can't get another job. There's no other boyfriend/girlfriend out there. I'm stuck"—and the pattern continues. Then things get progressively worse, and you wonder where your confidence went. You stopped having positive thoughts, and most important of all, you stopped having confidence. Why?

You lost control of your thoughts, thus closing the door on your confidence reserve. Your thoughts are powerful forces of energy. Thoughts create everything you want in life, and they affect your confidence and your courage. Thoughts can only come from your mind and you are ultimately the only person in charge of your own mind. It is the most powerful thing you can control. You create the thoughts that create the circumstances of your life.

Now that you know the "20 Steps to Get Rid of Negative Thinking" from chapter 5, you can determine your own thoughts. You're empowered. Empowerment means the promotion of self-actualization or influence. It means you are enabled to take an action, or have the freedom to do as you wish. We regulate our level of empowerment through our senses as well as through systematic efforts to gather relevant facts. We demonstrate our empowerment by our actions and our ability to communicate confidently.

Un-empowered, a player might think: "Should I tell the coach I feel I should be on the starting squad? Will he get mad and put me on the bench for speaking up?" Empowered, that same player will approach the coach and (hopefully with humility) be able to talk confidently.

Empowerment allows a person to communicate information in ways that are most effective and which best "make a point." He will be able to use words well, and he will know how to create effective ways to be understood.

For example, creating a graph is a way to give voice to your ideas. At work, at home, in speaking to teachers or to other people in positions of power, being able to chart information, to show a trend, or to manipulate data enables you to make your point visually. The ability to do so puts you in charge. Your ability to communicate your ideas, to persuade others to agree with your opinions improves as you become more empowered.

People who feel empowered can act with confidence, understand what they want, how to get what they want and are not afraid to communicate, to succeed, or even to fail. They see or relate to:

- The big picture—what story are their experiences telling them?

- The ideas within the big picture—where are the high points, the low points, the greatest change, no change? What are the relationships among and between past experiences? What do they want the outcome to be, and how this will increase their confidence reserve?

- The situational aspects—what do the signs tell them? What impact does the feeling or messages they are intuitively feeling have on their actions?

We are all empowered to follow our hearts and our minds. The confidence you gain from positive thinking will impact the level of empowerment that affects your follow through and actions.

ANXIETY

The opposite of confidence is anxiety. Anxiety is apprehensive uneasiness in a person's mind, usually over an impending or anticipated negative situation. Anxiety is an abnormal and overwhelming sense of apprehension and fear, often marked by physiological and physical signs (as sweating, tension, and increased pulse), doubt concerning the reality and nature of the threat, and self-doubt about one's capacity to cope with it.

Every person has a personal threshold for what they think they can handle. If pushed past this threshold by events, they feel stressed or overwhelmed. When a person tries pushing through their mental threshold of anxiety, the outcome can build confidence, and this adds to their reserve.

If a person suffered from an unusual situation or a lot of negative experiences growing up, he or she might develop a threshold that is lower than most people's. People and events will be more likely to push that person past this "lower than normal" threshold. When pushed to the brink of their threshold, people may initially exhibit a whole range of mental health conditions, including anxiety, anger, fear, depression, overeating, and substance abuse (to name just a few).

It's a lot like a football player who begins his training with a certain threshold for what he can handle physically, but by practicing every day, he pushes against that threshold, raising it to a point where he can now handle physically what would have overwhelmed him in the beginning. Thus his confidence is raised and anxiety is decreased.

FEAR

Fear is something completely different. Fear can even be used positively if managed correctly. You probably have good reason to be afraid when you have two 325-pound linemen running at full speed toward you with nasty intentions. My guess is that the fear you are feeling is going to motivate you to run just a bit faster than you would have otherwise. Suddenly you might discover you have moves you never knew about. Fear is the best motivator there is. We are all different and unique individuals. We are motivated by different things. The typical list of things people are motivated by can include:

- Potential Gain
- Being a hero
- Greed
- Convenience
- Comfort
- Security
- Pride of ownership.
- Satisfaction of
- Emotion
- Fear

Football teaches every young person how to face fear. It teaches them how to process the alternatives in a logical and reasonable way. It is pretty easy to process. "There are two guys twice my size running at me full speed with the intention of hitting me so hard I won't get up." The player quickly considers his options:

1. Freeze up, don't move, and get hammered

2. Fall to the ground before they get here and look like a coward

3. Run like hell

4. Make a few moves and try to make them miss

5. Call for mommy; she'll know what to do

If they chose number three or number four they probably did okay. If they were able to outrun these beasts or make them miss, they not only faced real fears, but also just added a little more to the confidence reserve compartment.

Some fears are real and useful. Other fears are just masked anxiety. If someone is driving 100 mph on a motorcycle and you're on the back, that's real fear. If someone has a gun to your head, that warrants fear. What you need to do is train your mind and yourself to process your fears.

THREE IMPORTANT QUESTIONS EVERYONE SHOULD ASK

Are the things or situations you are facing really something you should be afraid of, or is it just in your mind? The exercise and process you need to go through is to ask yourself, "What is the best and worst thing that could happen?" Take as much time as the situation allows and make a mental checklist of all the possible outcomes. One of the most fearful things to people is talking in front of a crowd. So let's use this for our example. You have just been asked to speak in front of two hundred strangers about your business. These people don't know you, don't your company, and have heard a thousand boring speeches before. How do you feel right this second? You might be confident because you have a few good situations in your reserve compartment, or you might be afraid. Your choices are:

- Give the speech and hope you are not a boring fool.

- Decline the opportunity and not worry about it.

Here's where the questions come in. What is the best thing that could happen if you pursue the opportunity to speak? The possible outcomes include:

- You are a big success.

- The crowd thinks you are brilliant.

- The group adores you.

- People find out about your business and want to work with you.

- You earn a lot of money from the referrals that came after the speech.

- You might find you have a future in public speaking.

- Someone in the crowd is so impressed they offer you a new higher-paying position.

- You get quoted in a trade magazine enhancing your exposure.

- Fame and fortune are within your reach.

Which one of the items on the above list doesn't feel good to you as a possible outcome? Just looking at this list trying to decide whether to pursue the opportunity to talk is easy. But are you still afraid? Fair enough.

The next question is: What is the worst thing that could happen?

WORST POSSIBLE OUTCOMES:

- You forget the material.

- You will be boring.

- You could make a fool out of yourself.

- You might not be very good.

- People might not like you.

- There could be someone the audience who knows more than you do and will expose your weaknesses.

All of these could happen. They are all logical and reasonable possibilities. So now what? If we just put the two lists next to each other you clearly see the possible positives far out weigh the potential negatives. Yes they do, but you are still scared. Your fear of looking like a fool outweighs the potential for greatness. So, the last of the three simple questions you need to ask yourself if you are facing a fearful situation is: What can I do to make sure the best things happen, not the worst?

Let's go back to our worst possible list and see if we can impact this list or have some control over making sure none of these things happen.

WORST POSSIBLE OUTCOMES:

- Forget the material. (Study, make notes that you will have with you.)

- Be boring. (Before the speech look for some jokes or clever antidotes.)

- Make a fool out of yourself. (Prepare and have conviction in what you are saying.)

- Not be very good. (Practice, practice, and practice some more.)

- People might not like you. (People might not like you if you don't do the speech.)

- Someone might be in the audience who knows more than you and will expose your weakness. (Nobody knows everything about everything. If someone does happen to know more than you, so what.)

Basically we can do things to ensure that the worst things won't happen. We have control over the outcome of this opportunity.

• What is the best thing that could happen?

• What is the worst thing that could happen?

• What can you do to make the best thing happen and not the worst?

If you have absolutely no control over whether the best thing could happen or the worst thing could happen, then you need to let it go because you are probably just having unwarranted anxiety and are not accessing your confidence reserve.

There is too much wasted energy and emotion worrying about what we can't control. There is enough things to process that you can control so let all the other ones go! The benefits of making a conscious effort to increase your confidence are endless. Increased confidence will help you:

- Talk up in a meeting.
- Speak in front of groups without worrying that you will make a fool of yourself.
- Feel good about yourself rather than knocking yourself down all of the time.
- Remove the self doubt and say "I can" rather than "I can't."
- Take some risks you are sure about.
- Stick up for yourself rather than let people walk all over you.
- Be able to say no!
- Decrease stress.
- Create fulfilling relationships.
- Improve your finances.
- Be more comfortable in social situations.

- Make accurate decisions.
- Meet people more easily.
- Express yourself with ease.
- Stop worrying.
- Enjoy inner peace.
- Succeed in business.
- Enjoy better health.
- Meet the perfect partner.
- Eliminate negative thoughts and feelings.
- Take charge of your life.
- Get a better job.
- Increase your salary.
- Make new and long-lasting friendships.
- Secure a promotion.
- Create and alter situations to what you want.
- Control your anxiety.

That's the short list of positives that having confidence will afford you. Now, make a list of all the ways not having confidence is or might be affecting your life today. Ask yourself the three questions above and see if you can't make a positive change today.

YOUR CONFIDENCE BUILDING PLAN

1. Do the "20 Steps to Get Rid of Negative Thinking" in chapter 5.

2. Review daily what you've accomplished by the end of the day that added to your confidence reserve. Don't minimize this

exercise. Give yourself a pep talk to start each day and end each day. Coach yourself and give yourself praise for your achievements regardless of how minor you might feel they are.

3. Look for inspiration always and often. The media is full of inspirational stories of tragedy to success. There are a lot of people that have it much worse than you. At times you might have to look to find them because you feel your situation is so overwhelming, but they are out there. If they (whoever "they" are) can overcome them so can you. The Arts & Entertainment channel has a show called *Biographies* that portrays notable individuals who rise, fall, and then rise again. Life happens to all of us and a life without challenges is called a "G" rated movie.

4. Volunteer

If you volunteer your time to help the less fortunate that will really put things in perspective for you. When you start comparing your situation and issues to the less-fortunate you might feel silly for being so down. You might find the strength that you need to integrate and execute all the secrets of football into your own life.

5. Bus the Right People

We have already discussed in previous chapters how important it is to get the right people on your mental bus and the wrong ones off. You need to surround yourself with people who will help build your confidence and limit your exposure to the ones that hold you down.

6. Push Yourself.

There is a saying in the south, "Fixin' to get ready." That means you are getting ready to do something, but you might not get around to actually following through. There are always reasonable-sounding justifications we can create for why we cannot do something. You need to push yourself. In my years of sales management it was an absolute that the worst sales people always had the best most creative justifications for why they were not making their numbers. I always thought that if they had put half as much thought and effort into selling as they did into their excuses for failing, they would succeed. If someone asked you to go out and run six miles, you might say you can't. You're too tired, too old, aren't a good runner, etc. But it all starts when we take the first step and it grows from there.

7. Set Goals

Don't expect results overnight, but do expect results. Make sure you have set reasonable time frames and expectations for yourself in improving your confidence. In order to have a reasonable time frame and expectations, you have to set goals for yourself. It is very important that you write these goals down somewhere they can be reviewed from time to time. A lot of people skip this step when they set goals. Writing them down helps your mind visualize them and gives you a stronger commitment to achieve them.

8. Keep Score

Hold yourself accountable. It is important to measure your progress because if you are not seeing the results you want and need, then it's time to review this chapter and see what adjustments you need to make.

There is a direct correlation to the effort you put into something and to the end result you receive. Thinking about building confidence, saying you are going to, but not measuring your progress and holding yourself accountable is like playing a football game, but not keeping score.

WEEKLY CONFIDENCE SCORE GRAPH

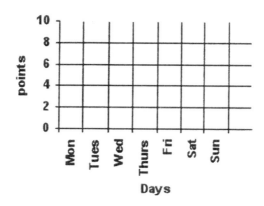

1. Give yourself one point for each action you do on any step of the "20 Steps to Get Rid of Negative Thinking." Keep track of your points.

2. At the end of the day, add up your points and plot the total for that day on a graph like the one above.

3. Make a Monthly Confidence Score Graph and use it to plot weekly-point totals. Watch your statistics rise and your confidence grow!

CHAPTER SEVEN

THE BATTLE
ON THE FIELD
COMPETITIVE SPIRIT

You never win a game unless you beat the guy in front of you. The score on the board doesn't mean a thing. That's for the fans. You've got to win the war with the man in front of you. You've got to get your man.

COACH VINCE LOMBARDI

123

Y ou must have a competitive spirit to compete in the game of football. When a mob of opposing players is trying to knock you to the ground, you develop this competitive spirit fast—or you fail. Boxing, basketball, hockey, and you-name-the-sport offer the same opportunity to develop competitive spirit but not at the same intensity as football. There is nothing like football to pump up your sense of competition—especially when the game is on the line. That's when a true competitor wants to take control of their destiny—and their rival's. You can witness this at just about any level of football, from peewee to pro.

When it is fourth-and-one from almost anywhere on the field, you will typically see the offense lobbying the coach to let them go for it. They believe they will make it. Their competitive nature fairly explodes. If you see an offense with this type of competitive spirit, you can bet they are going to succeed.

Rob was a sure bet the day he played an important conference game against the University of Nevada. It was one of those closely-fought battles with the lead changing hands several times. It was late in the fourth quarter. The momentum was with Nevada. Rob's team faced a critical fourth-and-one on their own forty-five-yard line with less than a minute left in the game. There was no choice but to go for it. Time-out was called before the play was selected, to make sure everyone on the offense knew their assignment. Rob pleaded with the coaches to give him the ball, which they had planned to do anyway.

He strapped up his team's football fortunes on his broad shoulders and barreled for not one yard, but *forty-one* yards! Now it was first-and-goal on the nine yard line. Rob wanted the ball again. On the very next play, as time ran out, he ran over at least three would-be tacklers to score the tying touchdown.

This put the game into an overtime situation. Nevada got the ball first. They managed a field goal to go ahead by three points.

Then Rice got its chance. Rob's team started twenty-five yards away from the goal line. The competitive spirit was alive and well! Rob got the call again. He answered in a big way. On the first play in overtime, he was hit in the backfield as soon as he was handed the ball. That didn't seem to deter him. He broke that tackle—and several more—on his twenty-five-yard winning touchdown run.

Rob scored not once, not twice, but three times that Saturday. The Rice University Owls came away with an improbable, 33 – 30 overtime victory.

It was wonderful to watch my son get so much recognition for his heroics. In a display of spontaneous exhilaration, Rob's teammates hoisted him up onto their shoulders and carried him off the field. As soon as the team let his feet touch the ground, Rob had a camera in his face, a microphone in his hand, and a long line of autograph-seekers calling his name.

Can you imagine how much your confidence reserve would rise as your teammates carried you off the field in a victory celebration? Rob led the WAC (Western Athletic Conference) in scoring at this point in the season. That's a great example of the competitive spirit and the first time in fifty years a Rice football player had been carried off the field, by his teammates!

CONSTANT OVERTIME

You and I might not have the same type of opportunity to show our competitive spirit, but the game of life is played in overtime every day. The contest always seems to be close and the outcome is almost always uncertain. So it is even more important that you take control and apply your inner competitive spirit to what you do, each and every day.

The way I look at competitive situations in business is simple: somebody is going to win or earn the business. It can be you or it can be your competition.

In business, I view the competition as the nastiest, ugliest, and most repulsive creature I can conjure up in my mind. Basically, what they are trying do is steal food off my table. They are reaching in my pocket, trying to take my money! Even worse: They are taking food right out of the mouths of my family! What am I going to do about this? I certainly do not sit back with a complacent attitude and justify it with you-win-some-you-lose-some attitude. I can make another choice: I play the business game with such a fierce competitive spirit that nothing less then winning 100 percent of the time satisfies me. You can too.

One of the tricks to winning is to always assume that you are losing. In the world of sales, I have seen far too many people drop the ball in the red zone (that's a football term for having the ball inside the opponent's twenty-yard line). They get near the goal line and feel certain they are going to score, so they let up a bit. Then, all of a sudden, they lose the opportunity to score because their competitor was working harder than they were to secure the business.

If you always assume you are losing, you will make sure every possible gap has been plugged, and there will be no surprises. How many times have you seen a football team that has gone ahead in a game by twenty-one points in the first quarter only to end up losing? It happens every week. If the team that was ahead played like they were behind by twenty-one points, they would never lose.

It is overtime every day, and you are behind in the game of life! If you instill that way of thinking, you will win much more often, and no one will be taking the food off your family's table.

$1,000,000 MISTAKE

An ex-football player and client of mine named Jack told me a story that illustrates this perfectly. Back in the early days of his business career, he was doing his usual cold-calling for new business. He came across an opportunity with a firm called Healthcare International based in Austin, Texas. Jack spoke to the decision-maker who told him that they had already pretty much decided to buy from Jack's competition.

The competition was much larger. That organization was ten times the size of Jack's. The decision-maker had never heard of Jack or his company. He was going to go ahead and make his decision to buy without even considering Jack's solution.

Being a fiercely competitive ex-football player, Jack couldn't let this happen. He applied his best logic to try to sway the decision-maker. He said, "You are going to make a $1,000,000 decision without looking at your best alternative. You will have to live with this decision for the next five or six years. Since you already have invested several months into your evaluation, what's a few more weeks? At least if you take a look at us, you'll be able to say you considered all the alternatives."

Jack was totally confident that if they would just look at his solution, he would have a chance. One thing he knew for certain was that if he *didn't* get this company to look at what he had to offer, he would have no chance whatsoever. After a few minutes, the decision maker replied, "Okay Jack. We'll come over to look at your product, but I want you to understand that we are coming over to disqualify you."

So Jack was at least in the game. He was way behind, more than twenty-one points in the fourth quarter, so to speak. He knew he'd better have a little more than a competitive spirit; he needed his A-game!

The Healthcare International (HI) team traveled to Jack's office. Jack's team unrolled their A-game in spades. HI was surprised at the professional presentation and the solutions that Jack's team provided. They were deeply impressed. They admitted that they could *not* disqualify Jack because everything he had told them about his product was true. They then invited Jack and his team to Austin to see their setup and meet more of their people.

All through the long selling process, Jack never let up. He maintained the viewpoint that he was always behind and had a lot of ground to cover.

During the meetings that took place over the next few months, Jack's passionate and competitive nature remained blazing hot. He knew he had an amazing opportunity. If he pulled this off, it would be the largest sale in his company's history. It would also mean that Jack would make his yearly sales-quota in one fell swoop.

To make a long story short, towards the end of the sales cycle, the decision-maker pulled Jack aside and leveled with him: "Jack there are only two reasons we agreed to look at your offering. The first reason was you—your passion, your logic, and your competitive spirit. You had so much conviction for what you were telling me I felt I had to take a look.

"The second reason—and honestly maybe the real driver—was that our team hated the other salesperson. He knew his company was the biggest. Because of that, he was arrogant and lazy. He didn't seem to want or need our business very badly. If he had been as aggressive as you, had your desire, and had shown your competitive spirit, we probably would not have even considered you."

Jack earned this $1,000,000 sale and beat the competition. It was not only his company's largest sale, it was the largest sale *in the industry to date for this type of product.* Jack earned a handsome six-figure commission check for his efforts. To this day, the "competitor" still doesn't know why he lost this account.

THE MORAL: Keep your competitive spirit alive and burning all the time!

COMPETITIVE INTELLIGENCE

Ask any football coach or business manager to define "competitive intelligence" and they'll probably tell you its "spy stuff" or that it's "industrial espionage." From the slightly better-informed, you'll hear fancier responses, like "it's a systematic collection and analysis of competitor's information." In its simplicity, it's finding out stuff about your opponents and using that information effectively.

However you define it, what competitive intelligence really boils down to a process and a product. The *process* consists of all the actions you take to get information about your competition. The *product* is what you decide to do with that information. Its value is priceless because with it, you are able to out-smart and out-maneuver your competition no matter if you're on the playing field, in the board room, or whenever you have to be competitive in life.

The scope of this information is broad. It involves more than simply understanding your competitor's behavior, although that is a key part. Its influence and usefulness shows up everywhere. If it's on a playing field, it not only guides your defence, it can subtly influence even the smallest decisions about a play. If it's in business, it influences everything from research and development of new products to everyday decisions about administration. Just know that, unlike industrial espionage, competitive intelligence is an ethical and legal business discipline widely utilized by both the business world and the world of football, and it can be useful to know how to do if you have to be competitive in other areas of your life.

All football teams—from high school on up—have scouts who go to watch other teams play. The scouts are there to track the opponents' tendencies in certain situations. Coaches and players spend countless hours pouring over the game films of their competitors so as to gather critical competitive intelligence. It is as important to their game planning as practice is.

In the business world, competitive intelligence has expanded from its early beginnings of helping a company win the zero-sum-game of "we-win-and-they-lose." Today it includes support thorough external information collection, analysis, and formulation of strategic recommendations, as well as virtually all of the sundry short- and long-term market objectives of a firm and its stockholders.

Competitive intelligence (CI) is an important part of any game plan. All football players and teams learn this fact early on, and competitive intelligence is the cornerstone to a winning team's weekly game plan. Used correctly, it can become the cornerstone of your game plan too.

In order to show you how competitive intelligence works, I'm going to stick with primarily how it works in business, throwing a little football in to keep it interesting. The mistake you can make as a competitive-intelligence scout is being nearsighted about a fact-finding mission. In the business world, CI scouts often define their own value to the firm as it relates to tracking competition in the near-term businesses against which the firm is currently competing. They make the mistake of not concentrating or directing any effort towards helping the firm to grow more profitable with the information they find or to take advantage of opportunities presented by economic circumstances.

At the other extreme, some competitive intelligence scouts expand their mission beyond these foundational priorities too quickly and try to influence future decisions of the business too much. A business cannot afford to become stuck in either the present or the future. The right balance of mission priorities is different for every firm and team; however, these priorities remain consistent in terms of the possibilities to incorporate the intelligence data acquired into a business game plan.

One very useful component of any competitive strategy is that it is vital for anyone during economic downturns (or for any team that does not have a winning record for that matter). It's also different in nature from the strategy you'd pursue during expansionary business cycles. For example, rather than expansion through marketing or production partnerships and licensing for new products—the typical business model in a strong economy—a competitive strategy might concentrate on capitalizing on the pain of one's smaller, cash-starved rivals—especially those with market capital invested in fast-growth markets that hold the future of the firm's diversified market strategy.

To illustrate the counter-intuitive nature of where competitive intelligence comes in, consider this: a company with a dominant position in a given market would logically throw up defenses to protect that core-market share from rivals. Most of these "rivals" couldn't launch an attack if they wanted to, often because of a lack of marketing resources. This approach is just like the football team that plays to protect a lead and loses their aggressive approach that got them the lead in the first place.

In fact, during contracting business cycles, a firm with a dominant market position (or a team with a large lead) should instead use an aggressive strategy. In business, that means applying more consistent cash-flow to finance a strategy that concentrates on maximizing the pain of smaller, weaker rivals in coveted markets. This strategy might mean acquiring some or forcing others out in order to dominate those markets when the business cycle recovers, as it inevitably will. This is a surprisingly little-used strategy, but one that—when applied with care—can result in a company emerging from an economic downturn stronger than ever. There is an abundance of similar lessons that "competitive intelligence" has to share.

LESS MEAT ON THE BONE
MEANS HUNGRIER COMPETITION

We've all heard the warning signs lately—rotton housing market, rising energy costs, stock market woes, layoffs beginning, industrial production slowing down, the Feds cutting interest rates. We're definatley experiencing an economic slowdown. Whether it's a protracted recessionary trend or a relatively brief downturn, one thing's for sure: if you thought you needed to watch competitors during boom times, think again. That was just a warm-up. Competitive forces will be *much* stronger for organizations when slower-growing markets result in less pickings to go around.

When there is less meat on the bone, everyone is hungrier, and this is where competitive intelligence becomes vital. You have to know what your competitors are doing as the market sinks. If you are going to succeed, you are forced to be proactive and even ruthless. Too many times, businesses start to sell scared and make the situation worse for themselves.

SCARCITY BREEDS RUTHLESSNESS

What all this means is that competitive intelligence and the resulting strategizing will become more important than ever as a cornerstone business discipline.

Businesses that were formerly comfortable in times of lame competition will be faced with the need to adapt to a slower-growing (or even shrinking) pie. These extremely competitive markets will drive conditions in the coming months and, possibly, years. This is the new economy. What will it mean for the businesses accustomed to competing for shares in markets where there was usually enough (relatively) easy money to go around for all players? Scarcity ultimately breeds ruthlessness.

THROTTLING COMPETITIVE PLANNING

Forces in the marketplace will cause every organization to either leave the market or compete more effectively for the scarcer dollars and slower growth that exists. They will accelerate their competitive strategies in order to capture the greatest advantage, no matter how long the slowdown lasts. Whether this year brings a mere slowdown in growth or a recession, companies are preparing for battle by releasing new products and services and intensifying efforts to boost the efficiency of their operations.

Increased efficiency will chiefly come through industry consolidation and by faster adoption of technological and managerial innovations. Differentiate or die, is the battle cry. Consolidation, buy-out or failure will be the sure fate of those who ignore the need to be more aggressive and change their approach.

During a slowdown, increased competition makes it tougher for all players to turn a profit and attract slower-growing market demand to eat up their supply. The shakeout that follows forces out the weakest competitors. This same shakeout also makes the strongest even stronger. The surviving companies become even more efficient as markets become more profitable for those left standing. Like the change of seasons in nature, the business cycle separates the weak from the strong. Only the strong survive.

Understand and assume your role as a successful competitive-intellegence scout in your own business, and utilize the strategies to your advantage. It doesn't have to be difficult. Just remember, competitive intelligence is simply another example of how strategies that apply to the game of football spill over to the world outside of sports.

MINIMIZING THREATS

Competitive intelligence has always concentrated its attention on minimizing threats, whether in football or business. It does this through encouraging a better understanding of the shorter-term operational initiatives a team or firm might take to dominate the markets in which the company currently operates relative to its competitors for that same market.

Football teams and businesses are both steeped in winning. They both focus on building effective competitive-intelligence data. They both have the mission of remaining aware and responsive to competitive threats as they arise on the field or in the marketplace. This rather reactionary perspective remains competitive intelligence's primary objective.

Often you'll hear more "proactive" thinkers discount and deride this simple objective of being aware of current activities in a marketplace. Likewise they will downgrade the value of knowing an opponent's probable game plan. I would argue that these are the minimum that must be done to craft an effective competitive strategy in the short-term.

Maximizing Opportunities

The most common area in which new competitive intelligence functions disappoint its internal customers is that they fail to maximize new business opportunities for the firm. This may be due to the many managers who refuse to accept competitive intelligence's role in helping their company select new markets for existing offerings—the "low-hanging fruit." Some of these same managers also refuse to develop fresh revenue streams and other opportunities the firm needs in order to grow value for its shareholders.

There is a vital lesson competitive intelligence scouts need to learn: their value will best be judged on the basis of how much they actually contribute to the net profitability of the enterprise at large.

A successful football team must change its offensive and defensive schemes week in and week out, so they don't become predictable to their opponents.

It is far more important for the competitive intelligence personnel to help the team or firm find new opportunities for existing or adapted plays or products. In its role, competitive intelligence can often help move the organization towards its most profitable potential direction, while also helping the company avoid costly and sometimes ruinous mistakes in strategic direction made by decision makers higher-up.

A football team complacent in their strategy loses their competitive edge and will have a hard time winning. The same holds true for a business or an individual. Think of competitive intelligence as an aggressive and opportunistic exercise, rather than a defensive, status-quo protection activity. That's how football scouts think when they watch rival teams. This philosophical approach becomes just one of a dozen more diverse missions that the most advanced and well-developed intelligence teams are charged with. Indeed, those competitive intelligence scouts who think this way usually drop the "competitive" part of competitive intelligence. They become, much as government intelligence programs do, a more general and broadly commissioned function that provides the backbone of decision-making and due diligence for the firm or team.

The list below describes these priorities in rough order of levels of sophistication and relative importance to the average enterprise. It is uncanny how similar it is to what an effective football team has to gather. This same list works very well when used as steps to become your own competitive intelligence scout.

While not intended to be comprehensive, this list does establish boundaries and areas by which any competitive intelligence scout can help influence the future expansion of his organization or team by continuously increasing value-added results for his organization or team. Similarly, such a diversification strategy will increase its own product or market offerings to deliver value to a broader customer base.

1. CURRENT COMPETITOR ACTIVITIES & STRATEGY GATHERING

The standard meat of a competitive intelligence program is to be aware and helpful in understanding competitors' current activities and plans. Usual sources for this kind of research come from public announcements (web, clients, news, PR, etc.) and follow-up interviews conducted with the competitor. This data is best used to ascertain their commitment to current initiatives. In the game of football this would include game films from other teams and also conversations among non-competing scouts, and coaches. This is standard, old-school "competitor intelligence." It's the constant striving to know how to successfully transfer market share from the competitor's company to one's own. In football, it means being to be able to predict your opponent's strategy on game day.

2. CUSTOMER AND VENDOR MONITORING

Threats of backwards-and forwards-integration by customers and vendors is a possibility often discounted, but it is a fact most often realized by firms every day. An understanding of customer-base selling or the "Cash Cow" can be revealing in terms of unexploited opportunities to sell more products or services within existing customer relationships, thereby minimizing selling and marketing costs while maximizing impact within a customer's value chain. This also serves to exclude competitors from those self-same opportunities. Many times the difference between a win and a loss is finding unexploited opportunities for new plays, or testing your opponent's potential vulnerabilities.

3. OPERATIONAL OR PERFORMANCE BENCHMARKING

Benchmarking initiatives—evaluating the best practices companies do—are traditionally conducted against direct competitors. These can also prove beneficial in studying competitors, as well as best-in-class or best-in-world firms that can easily move into diversified businesses to take advantage of market opportunities perceived by their own intelligence team. Most often, such benchmarking studies begin by isolating the operational deficiencies present in the firm and identifying practices at firms that excel in those areas. The next step is conducting research to determine why they excel. The researching firm can then transfer that knowledge to its own group to increase tactical efficiency. Analyzing these win/loss reports is a traditional way to gather benchmarking data. This is closely tied to an understanding of the concept known as "core competence." Core competence contains those characteristics that are competitively unique and contribute a disproportionate share of customer-perceived value. The core competencies enable the firm to use these same characteristics to expand into new markets. Sometimes a company can catch up with a competitor or develop their own differential compared to other supplier options that will create a level of market dominance based on operational efficiency. In terms of football: oftentimes competing football teams have played each other before. Teams all review their play charts to see what worked and what didn't, so they won't make the same mistakes again. They also study the charts to find successful plays they can use again. Lots of statistical data is counted to determine a team's operational efficiency.

4. BATTLE PLANNING

The future is the battleground for any game and for all business. As we try to predict the future, "scenario planning" is a tool many competitive strategists use both in business and football. Scenario planning allows a firm to understand the total of all possible futures and assign probable likelihood to each of those possibilities, thereby gaining an understanding of what is likely to happen. Football and business battle plans try to predict how companies or teams will make decisions, and what the comparative outcomes of those decisions will be across a number of quarters. For example: where they will invest, what markets they will attack, which ones will they abandon, what play will they call in certain situations, etc.

5. SALES & MARKETING SUPPORT

One of the highest-impact areas that the intelligence scouts can assist in is a solid understanding of the strengths and weaknesses of competitor's and of the firm's own customers. Market perceptions, helping the sales force win new customers, or maximizing their share of existing ones can be the make-or-break item. While the ability to contribute recommendations to a sales force for ensuring the "FUD-Factor" (fear, uncertainty and doubt) in the minds of customers about competitors' products and services is important, it's also critical to understand the marketing messages relayed to this customer-base by competitors. This understanding can help the firm mitigate threats to existing customers and win more profitable revenues from new ones.

6. KNOWLEDGE DISSEMINATION

Knowledge dissemination and its connection with competitive intelligence has often been talked about. Some 80 percent of what a team needs to know about its competitors already exists within the team. It's important to offer assistance to the competitive intelligence scouts to exploit these internal sources. In business, at every sales meeting for example, assign certain individuals to a competitor. This individual would gather data all year long and then present his or her findings to the rest of the team. In the realm of professional football it could work this way: players switch teams often at this level. The knowledge a player might have about his old team can be invaluable.

7. MERGERS &ACQUISITIONS: ALLIANCE-INVESTMENT SUPPORT

Buying, investing in and allying with companies that have something to offer—either in the form of marketing channels or product capabilities—provides many firms the engine of growth for their future expansion. However, statistically speaking, most deals fail to produce the highly touted and endlessly promised shareholder value they purport to deliver. This is most often due to a lack of due diligence in the qualification process. Recent efforts to include pre-deal due diligence by competitive intelligence teams have had substantial effects on post-deal success, beginning with selection of candidates and ending with final consummation of the deal and integration of enterprises.

8. MARKET PROSPECTS

Are you in the right business—today? Tomorrow? That's what an understanding of market prospects can produce for your firm. Every business is locked into the endless loop of the "product life cycle" that includes not only the most profitable periods of product or service lifespan, but also eventual decline and death. This is most commonly directed towards understanding which markets will be fastest-growing and then making recommendations to decision-makers on the means by which the firm can come to dominate those markets. A solid understanding of core competence is also important here. Riding a core product too long without making timely changes has led to the downfall of innumerable organizations.

9. LEGISLATIVE/REGULATORY IMPACT ON BUSINESS ISSUES

In certain industries more than others, government activities in both legislative and regulatory compliance can be disproportionately influential in enabling or hobbling a firm's competitive strategy. Typically this is most influential in industries for the public interest such as telecom, finance, energy, healthcare and transportation. Another situation can arise if a certain drug or market strategy meets with regulatory scrutiny—witness the recent energy-availability concerns in the USA. Legal issues can and often do ensue, effectively scuttling the competitive strategies of the market players involved.

This occurrence must be planned for, despite the relatively small likelihood of outcome.

10. CONSULTATIVE BRIEFINGS

This is the catch-all final category. Intelligence scouts are required to assist both tactical and strategic decision-makers in becoming aware of all options available to them. This is true in football and in business. The real value-add that most managers or coaches ask for when they request better information is simply a more thorough understanding of the options available to them. They don't want to miss any options that they might not have thought of on their own. These "trusted-advisor" missions are diverse and require the most highly developed understanding of one's own intelligence mission and resources. These consultations also provide the greatest opportunity for the intelligence scouts to make an impact on the company's long-term competitiveness. Likewise, the penultimate objective of every intelligence function should be to become a highly trusted advisor. We spend considerable time in our training courses helping organizations understand how to become trusted advisors to prospects and the incredible value therein.

Ultimately, competitive information is still about understanding what is likely to happen, predicting outcomes with a reliable degree of accuracy, and devising a pre-defined response or countervailing strategy to minimize the impact of such events to the company. At its most fundamental level, to ensure continued success, competitive intelligence must provide an awareness of the current marketplace drivers and competitive forces.

WHAT'S YOUR SIGN?

Rice's University football team learned a hard lesson about competitive intelligence. Rice coaches have a system where they call in plays with hand signals to the players on the field. The Rice offense will move into position on the line of scrimmage with no played called. The coaches then look to see how the opposing defensive players lined up. Once they see the defensive alignment, the Rice coaches signal in the play to the offense. Everyone on the offense knows what the signals mean and respond accordingly.

This is a brilliant strategy. If you ever played electric football as a kid, you can really appreciate the brilliance of this tactic. For those of you who have never seen the game of electric football, it is *just* like real football, kind of. The game is played on a miniature vibrating metal football field about half the size of a small card table. Because it vibrates, the football field makes your players move—they kind of jitterbug across the hash marks.

You have eleven offensive players. Your opponent has eleven defensive players. Each person lines up his team. Then you turn on the switch. The metal vibrates and all the players begin to move. As soon as any of the defensive players bumps into the offensive player with the ball, the play is over. But here's a tactic that really makes winning easier: it is a lot easier to score if you let your defensive opponent place all of his plastic players in position *before* you set up your offense. Once you see how the defense is aligned, you can stack all your offensive players on one side. The ball carrier is then protected by ten blockers. He can jitterbug to the goal line untouched and thus score with ease. It doesn't work quite like that in a real football game; however, knowing how the defense is lining up really helps the offense call the right play.

At this particular football game, everyone in the stands noticed the opposing team's defensive players looking at the Rice coaches before each play. Somehow this defense gave the Rice offense trouble all day. Rice ended up losing this game by a last-minute field goal. This loss was particularly tough since it put any chance for post-season play out of their reach.

After the game, one member of the opposing team told a Rice player that the defense knew what play the Rice offense was going to run because they could read most of the Rice coaches' hand signals. They knew what plays were coming! Of course they were going to win with an advantage like that! Prior to the game, this team had really done their competitive intelligence gathering. This intelligence gathering was the major factor that gave Rice's opponents a victory that day. The proof is that Rice had never lost to this team before.

It's Up to You

As an individual or as an organization, you have to employ a competitive spirit if you are going to survive and win. Gathering, analyzing, and using competitive information is just a subset of the competitiveness it takes to succeed in the world we live in today. As an individual you can't count on anyone but yourself to acquire this knowledge. Some organizations offer this type of information on a silver platter to their people. If so, be smart enough to use it, update it, and validate it. If you're not given this information, then know you need to budget your own time to gather whatever information you need in order to create a competitive advantage.

You have to want more than just your fair share of the meat on the bone. Successful football players and teams don't just want to win *some* of their games. No. They go into *every* game wanting (and expecting) to win. And if you expect to win, you will have to develop a ruthless attitude. You will have to learn to want *all* the meat on that bone! Things are never equal. Each time someone goes into a situation with an advantage. It really is your choice whether that advantage belongs to you or to your competitor. A survival hint: Make sure it's yours!

CHAPTER EIGHT

IN THE ZONE

FOCUS

The man who succeeds above his fellow man is the one who early in life clearly discerns his objective, and towards that objective he directs all of his powers.

COACH VINCE LOMBARDI

JOCK OF ALL TRADES

How many people can you name who have excelled in multiple sports on a professional level? I can name three: Jim Thorpe, Bo Jackson and Dion Saunders. There are probably more, but the point is that there are not very many. The reason is simple. It is hard to do too many things at once. If an athlete, an individual outside of athletics, or even an organization tries to focus on too many things, they usually will not excel at anything. At best, they end up doing a lot of things at an average level.

Average won't get any of us very far, especially in the world we live in today. We are all forced to specialize, to become experts in specific fields. Doctors today specialize in one particular area of medicine (heart, brain, feet, etc.), high-end attorneys practice law in only one area (domestic, real-estate, criminal, civil, etc.), sales professionals concentrate their skills in a specific area (technical sales, account sales, tele-sales, product sales, etc.).

Knowledge is being generated at a tremendous rate of speed. Because there is so much more information available today, no one has the time to know everything. I'm sure you've met some people who act as if they know it all. You know the person who has an answer for everything, but no practical experience to back up the information he or she gives you. Rarely are these people really successful or truly focused.

Think of some successful people, especially those in athletics. They developed focus for their sport early in their life. They are proof that the sooner we can figure out what we want, the better. Golfer Tiger Woods is a perfect example. I've seen videos of Tiger with a golf club in his hand at the age of three with his dad standing by his side, helping him learn the game. You might even recall the show *That's Incredible* with hosts Fran Tarkington,

John Davidson and Cathy Lee Crosby. Each week on this one-hour primetime TV show, they would introduce us to incredible acts, feats, and people from around the world. One of the people they featured was Tiger Woods, when he was about six or seven. At that tender age, Tiger was already shooting golf scores that would embarrass most of us weekend hackers. He went on to become the number one player in the world and will likely be so for many years to come. Tiger Woods is focused, and he has been for his entire life.

The number one female tennis players in the world are the Williams sisters, Venus and Serena. Their success story parallels Tiger's. They started focusing on tennis early in their childhood. Through practice, determination, and the support of their parents, they have reached the pinnacle of their sport as well. There are many athletes like Tiger Woods and the Williams sisters. Rest assured, they all followed the principles you are reading about in this book. One common denominator for all of them is their ability to focus. They have to focus early and always, just like you and I can learn to do.

Football, as I have mentioned, is a very demanding sport. If you are going to be at the top of your game, you need a year-round commitment. A player has to focus their efforts for the other nine months a year in order to compete at a high level during the three-month season. Even during the season a player's work and focus continues. The preparation never ends until you quit playing. Players need to lift weights, run, watch film, stretch, and a whole host of other activities. And this does not just pertain to the professional or college-level athletes. Even high school players who want to move up to the next echelon must develop the same type of focus.

The more you can focus on one area of expertise, the more success you will have. Take Willy Shoemaker, for example. He was one of the most successful jockeys ever to ride a horse. There was a milk ad several years ago showing Willey standing next to Wilt Chamberlain, one of the greatest basketball players of all time. How do you think Willy would have done if he'd tried to play basketball when the horseracing season was over? He would have failed miserably. If he hadn't focused on horseracing, he wouldn't have been a success as a Jockey.

Do you remember when Michael Jordan tried to play baseball? Not many people would debate that MJ was one of the best athletes of this or any century. Even with all his skills and talents, he couldn't succeed in two sports. After a few seasons of being a mediocre baseball player, Michael put the bat and glove away and concentrated on being the best basketball player in the NBA. Sure, he could have continued to play both basketball and baseball, but his status as a superstar NBA player would have suffered due to lack of focus.

PICK A LANE

We need to be able to pick a lane and stick with it. You can't focus on too many things and do them all well. It is very important that you understand this concept. It's evident everywhere you look—at home, at work, at school.

As an example, Rice University's rushing offense has been consistently one of the top ten in the nation. This includes powerhouse universities like Nebraska, Oklahoma, Miami, USC, and all the other schools you are familiar with. In no small measure, it's due to Coach Ken Hatfield's ability to focus.

During the time Rob was at Rice, Coach Hatfield was the fifth most-winning active college-football coach in the USA. He'd coached at the Air Force Academy, won a national Championship at Arkansas, and headed the football program at Rice for fourteen years. His career as a football coach spanned more than thirty years.

If you visit Rice's competitive football program and watch Coach Hatfield at work, you can see how he focuses only on his job. Of course, as the head of a major college football program, he does have a full staff to clear the way for him. Let's dig into this a little bit.

First, there's his coaching staff. A team always has multiple coaches. They each focus on their areas of expertise. There is typically an offensive line coach, a defensive line coach, a running back coach, a defensive back coach, a receiver coach, a linebacker coach, an offensive coordinator, a quarterback coach, a special teams coach and a defensive coordinator, just to name a few. All of these coaches are responsible for specific areas.

You might ask, "Why can't the defensive coach just coach the entire defense?" Or, "If Coach Hatfield is such a good coach, why does he need all these other coaches." The reasons center around focus! A defensive back has a much different skill set, responsibilities, and duties than a defensive lineman. You need different coaches with different levels of expertise to focus on helping make sure the best players, best game plan, and the best team strategy for their areas are all set up and executed. Coach Hatfield, with all of his wins and experience can't see everything, know everything and be everywhere all at once. This includes the details on and off the field.

To even get ready to play, Coach Hatfield needs a small army of people. There is the equipment manager who gets all the equipment to the games, sets up the lockers, and makes sure everything is ready for the team. There's the medical staff who tapes up the players, tends to injuries, and makes sure the team is as healthy as possible. There is the marketing staff who coordinates all the radio and TV coverage and the communication between the schools. There are people to announce the games, keep the stats, make the travel arrangements, raise money for the program, work with the alumni, work with the boosters, film the games, and the list goes on and on. When you think about it, there are a staggering amount of details that have to be attended to in order to prepare for a high-level football contest. In some cases, there can be more than a hundred people involved. And if the game is on the road, then the details just multiply, making the event even more challenging.

How possible would it be for Coach Hatfield to focus on the game plan if he had to think about whether his linebacker's shoulder pads were repaired and returned after the last game? Or, did the last game's winning trophy make it home to the trophy case? He might be able to do all these varied tasks, but if he did, he'd be taking some of his focus off the critical items that determine whether the Rice team wins or loses. Coach Hatfield knows how to pick a lane and focus on what he does best. Focus is what ensures the best results for his team.

Too many times, people try to focus on too many things at once. They try to please too many people at once. If you try to make everyone on your mental bus happy, you'll likely end up making no one happy, including yourself. Decide and focus on what you do best. Focus on the important things and don't sweat the small stuff. Life is too short. You'll never reach your full potential unless you focus and pick a lane—and then focus in even more.

Coach Hatfield chose to perfect one particular play called the triple option offense. This laser-beam focus is what made it possible for Rice University's football team to remain one of the top rushing offenses in the nation, year in and year out.

The classic triple option is where the quarterback has the choice to give the ball to the fullback to run up the middle, run the ball himself around the end, or pitch it to a trailing halfback. There are many variations and formations on the triple option. It is very confusing to defend. A lot of times, whether you are on the field or in the stands, you have no idea who actually has the ball. In other words, the triple option is football's version of the shell game.

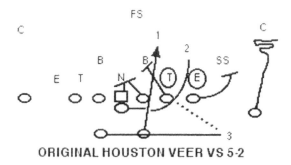

ORIGINAL HOUSTON VEER VS 5-2

THE TRIPLE OPTION

When I watched Rice games, there were many times I was certain the fullback had the ball, only to suddenly see the quarterback sprinting around the end. Above is an illustration what this play looks like drawn on the chalkboard.

If it's that hard to see from the stands who has the ball, you can only imagine what it must like on the field. Combining football's shell game with a three-hundred-pound lineman trying to decide who to tackle makes the triple option an effective rushing strategy. This is all quite difficult to manage if you are a defensive coordinator on the opposing squad.

No team in America ran the triple option better than Rice, under Coach Hatfield. I don't think many people would argue whether Coach Hatfield knows the triple option better than anyone coaching the game of football. Coach Hatfield knows he has an advantage with his unique knowledge of this offensive scheme. The players practice the triple option hundreds of times, until they are experts in it.

There are a lot of things that have to happen for this running play to work. The quarterback has to read the defensive end and the linebackers. Then the QB has to decide whether to give the ball to the fullback or pull it back. The correct read can be the difference between a touchdown or yardage lost. If the quarterback decides to pull the ball back, he has to determine whether to run it himself or pitch the ball to the tailback. He also has to know when exactly to pitch it. If he pitches it too early, the play will be a bust. A bad pitch can result in a fumble and a complete change in the momentum of the game.

The triple option requires superb timing and focused athletes to run it correctly. There is another aspect as well. The practice required between the fullback and the quarterback is intense. When the play is called in the huddle, the fullback does not know if he is getting the ball or not. The determination is made when the fullback is running full speed into the line. The quarterback actually places the ball in the fullback's stomach and then—if he sees there is no opening in the line—pulls it back. The "mesh," as it is referred to, is the timing and the feel between the quarterback and his fullback. This is the most difficult and critical part of the triple option. If the fullback takes the ball when the quarterback was going to pull it, there can be a fumble or a busted play. If he doesn't clamp down on the ball when the quarterback gives it to him, another set of disasters can happen. You can see why only a few teams use this offensive approach as their bread and butter.

Coach Hatfield figured out how to make the triple option work for the Rice football team. He focused his offensive game plan on this specific play and leveraged it to develop his teams into a national competitor. This is a lesson we all need to pay attention to. If you are not immediately sure of what you do best—what unique skills, knowledge or talents you possess—then you need to focus. You need to determine what your skills and talents are. Then it will become easy for you to pick a lane, just like Coach Hatfield did.

We all have special God-given talents. Some people have more than others, but we all have them. For some it might take a lifetime to determine what they are. Some people never discover their true talents. The consequence for these people is a life unfulfilled. They never realize their full potential. They tend to struggle, switching jobs or careers every couple of years in search of something they are missing. Sometimes it's like trying to cram a square peg into a round hole. Sure, you can pound the square peg in until it fits, but it's never perfect. It never feels quite right.

To help you determine what you should focus on, make a list of things that come easily to you. We often take for granted what is easy for us. Because it is easy for us, we think it must be easy for everyone. That is not the case at all. As an example, my dad is very handy. He can fix things, build things, and put just about anything together. I, on the other hand, would rather have rope burns than do some of the projects he can handle blindfolded. I think my father takes his unique talent in this area for granted. He has never leveraged those talents in his career.

I know my limitations. The times I have tried building or putting something together have always resulted in a frustrating experience for me. I learned quickly to hire someone for that type of work. It is just as important to know what you are not good at as it is to know what your unique skills and talents are.

Focus Factor Chart

Here is a simple exercise to determine what talents you should focus on and what you should leave to others. You are going to take a slice of your day and break it into time segments. Then you are going to chart and grade your activities.

Before you make your own, look at the following sample Focus Factor Chart.

Sample Focus Factor Chart

ACTIVITY	AMOUNT OF TIME SPENT	DEGREE OF DIFFICULTY	HAPPINESS FACTOR	MOVING ME FORWARD
Went for a run	1 hour	5	8	2
Worked on computer	2 hours	2	8	5
Made cold calls for new prospects	4 hours	1	1	6
Sat in meeting	2 hours	7	3	5
Wrote in book	2 hours	9	9	6
Played video games	3 hours	9	9	1
Talked to friends on line	1hour	9	7	2

Look at this hypothetical chart for salesperson Jane Doe. She seems to dislike cold calling and she hates meetings. Yet she spends the bulk of her time doing these activities. She may have rated these activities as a five or six for moving herself forward because her current job is selling. These are required activities for her profession, and they will, in theory, move her towards success. However, these activities may not move her to where she'd really like to be.

A simple analysis of this one-day chart might tell Jane that she would be more fulfilled and happier if she were a computer technician or an author. A close look would show that she spends six of the fifteen hours in her day doing things she didn't like. That represents 40 percent of her time. She spends another four hours on unproductive activities, which represents another 27 percent of her time. So in total, she spends 67 percent of her time doing either unproductive activities or activities she doesn't enjoy. Wake up, Jane! Life is too short to spend in misery, not pursuing your life's dream.

If *you* diligently fill out your own Focus Factor Chart for thirty to ninety days, you will see patterns in *your* life. You are empowered to change these patterns. You can create the path that will focus your talents, desires, and actions.

Okay. Follow the directions below and make your own chart.

1. Write the following column headings: Activity; Amount of time spent on the activity; Degree of activity difficulty; Happiness factor; and whether the activity is moving you closer to where you want to be.

2. Fill in your chart. Enter each activity. Record the time you spend doing each activity.

3. Grade each activity according to Difficulty, Happiness Factor etc. A "1" would be the lowest grade, the least productive, the unhappiest; a "10" would be the highest grade, the most productive, the happiest. After you've graded each activity you'll see the amount of time you spend on activities you don't enjoy. These activities keep you or put you in a rut.

Maybe you have done this first step before in some version—perhaps the first step of a diet plan. Many diets ask you to write down everything you consume. It is amazing how much junk we eat and don't even realize it. Once you write this list and are accountable for the food you eat, it becomes easy to see why you are gaining or losing weight.

In the game of football, it is a little easier to figure out your strengths and weaknesses. Once you determine those, some of your career choices become pretty evident. For instance, if you weigh three hundred pounds and run a forty yard dash in 5.5 seconds, there's not much chance you will become a running back. You will likely be better on the line. The reverse is true as well: a one hundred and fifty-pound player will get run over if he tries to be a guard or a tackle. (Unless you're about ten years old.)

As you read this, it is easy to understand the logic behind these thoughts. In the real world, it is not so easy. Oftentimes, we get so wrapped up in life's daily struggles that we end up in an unsuccessful position that is not suited for us, leaving us unfulfilled.

WHAT YOU DO IN PRACTICE, YOU'LL DO IN THE GAME

"What you do in practice you'll do in the game" is a common phrase used by football coaches to teach their players. If you quit on blocks, loaf, lose concentration, don't run hard, etc. in practice, you'll do the same on game day. Bad habits carry over. In the game of life, there is no practice field. You are in the game of life everyday. As part of your normal routine, you can choose to incorporate good habits and eliminate bad habits.

Here's how: identify any bad habits you might have formed that are lessening your productivity or holding you back. For example, playing video games, drinking, watching TV, going to movies, etc. are all potential good stress-relieving activities. We all need enjoyable outlets that help us to relax. The key is to insure moderation. If you find in your Focus Factor Chart that you spend an unbalanced amount of your time in leisure activities, then you probably aren't making enough progress or pushing yourself hard enough to reach your full potential. Remember: actions speak louder than words. You might say that you are going to break any bad habits, but until you do, it's only noise.

You might not have coaches around you correcting your mistakes, pushing you to achieve and pointing out your bad habits. But you do have friends around who—if you ask them—will tell you what they perceive your bad habits or practices might be.

Sometimes it's painful to hear their answers. But if you ask for help from people you love and respect, they will more likely than not tell you where they think you might be falling down a bit. To ask for this type of evaluation, you have to be open-minded and not be defensive. Otherwise, the information they offer you will be lost. Famous author Oliver Wendell Holmes is quoted as saying, "We all need education in the obvious." Let's make a short list of possible bad habits:

- Sleeping in
- Procrastinating
- Not thinking of others
- Taking and not giving
- Being negative
- Being too sarcastic
- Not being supportive
- Lying
- Cheating
- Stealing
- Not being responsible
- Acting like a know-it-all
- Not listening
- Just getting by
- Settling for average
- Being disrespectful
- Lack of attention to detail
- Being rude
- Being obnoxious
- Eating poorly
- Wasteful spending
- Being too emotional
- Control freak
- Being late
- Being unhealthy
- Bad-mouthing others
- Not trying
- Not communicating
- Not helping
- Being arrogant
- Being unproductive
- Being hurtful
- Not being considerate
- Drinking too much

No one is perfect. I'm sure there are times you have been or done at least one or two things on this list. If any of these—or the thousands of additional ones we could add—are part of your normal routine, you have developed some bad habits. This means there is some work to be done. You need to consider changing some aspects of your life! Changing your mindset and actions *will* change your life. Whether an athlete or not, successful people practice good habits. Regardless of what your habits are today, you can improve. Strive to be all you can be and welcome the opportunity to evolve. Life is a journey. It's yours to enjoy.

ACT AS IF.....

If you've done your own Focus Factor Chart, you now know a little bit more about how you spend your time. You've identified some bad habits you want to change. You have a better idea of what you want to do. Now you can focus on how to get to your ideal scene.

One day I was listening to the radio on my way home from work. It was a sports-radio talk show, and the host was discussing the 2000 Olympic games. The announcer was talking about how successful athletes perform active visualization to help them focus. I had never heard of active visualization, so I was intrigued. He explained that many of the athletes close their eyes prior to their event and think about the outcome they want. They actually play the event in their mind, like a movie. They visualize the outcome, frame by frame. They see themselves coming across the finish line in first place. To them, the contest is already over—and they have already won.

This sounded interesting to me. I thought I would have the kids give it a try on the way to one of their Pop Warner football games. To be honest, I also thought it would also be an excellent way to get some peace and quiet in a car loaded with young boys. I told my players to close their eyes and think about what the first play might be. I instructed them to think about getting the ball, about people trying to tackle them, about going through every move, etc. After they mentally walked through a couple of plays, I told them to work through the entire game. It not only gave me some peace and quiet on the drive, it also helped the players to have a better game that day.

VISUALIZING POSITIVE OUTCOMES

If you ever have a chance to speak with a professional athlete or a world-class Olympian, ask them about visualization. They will share their experiences. Better than that, try it for yourself.

CHECK IT OUT

Here's an exercise you can do to demonstrate another aspect of "acting as if." This exercise will also strengthen your ability to set goals, which we talked about in chapter 3. Whether you are an aspiring NFL player or you're looking for a new job, it is a successful action to write down exactly what you want to happen or the direction you want your life to go.

So, write it down! Then, determine how much you would like to earn in this endeavor. There are very few limits here. Be reasonably crazy. No one but you will know the amount. There's nobody around to laugh at you—just go for it! Next, write yourself a check for that amount. Consider this check a prepayment for future services or accomplishments.

Go ahead. Write the check. Then put it in your desk drawer and pull it out every so often. What would your life be like if you could really receive a check like that? How different would things be for you? Start visualizing that new life.

This exercise may seem a little over the top, but try it. What do you have to lose? First of all, it's a lot of fun. But, hey, even if it's not fun, that's okay, too. Maybe you'll get so frustrated you will be motivated to take the necessary steps to change. Either way, this exercise can push you in the right direction or will assist you to see who you want to be, what you want to do, and what you want to have. It will certainly help to think in this "as if…" mode. If you don't think "as if…," if you don't reach for the brass ring, forget it. You'll have no chance.

Thinking "as if …" is the first step (in other words, conception). The next step is acting "as if…"(or belief). Then the only thing remaining is putting your conception and belief into action so you can achieve the results you want. At the end of the day, that is up to you. You're only restricted by the limitations you put on yourself.

TRIPLE OPTION OF LIFE

Life's Purpose

FAMILY   CAREER

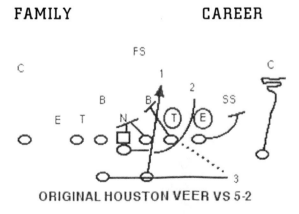

ORIGINAL HOUSTON VEER VS 5-2

You have already seen the diagram of the triple option play for football. Above is your triple option for life. This play is the most important for you.

It has a lot of similarity to the football play. In life you have to make quick decisions. How good those decisions are will determine the success you have. You can also fumble in life. You probably have at one time or another. I certainly have. But we all need to be able to read situations or create the best situation for ourselves. Again this is just like the football triple option play.

YOUR LIFE'S PURPOSE

Albert Einstein said, "Try not to become a man of success, but rather become a man of value."

Maybe you are reading this book to help determine what your life's purpose is. Good for you. The unique qualities you possess will help you determine your life's purpose and set your direction. No two people are the same; however, most people in this world share essential personal ethical principles and values. These principles and values guide them in their life path.

The most successful people are highly value-oriented. Their life's purpose is as strong as they value their position, their responsibilities to themselves and to the people around them. The people you encounter will like and respect you for your value orientation. Whether it's in sports or business, your value orientation also impacts the level of respect you receive. Let me explain further:

The people on your football team or in your business are counting on you to do your absolute best at executing your responsibilities. There are always opportunities to take short cuts, to just do enough to get by, or to delegate tasks that you should do on your own. This is a self-serving and selfish approach. A person can get away with this type of operating basis for a while, but it will catch up with them. At the end of the day, there are no secrets. Eventually people find out.

Your personal integrity and your values determine what type of professional you are. Sure, one of the definitions of a "professional" is anyone who gets paid for services rendered. If that is the definition we are going to use, then even a prostitute can be referred to as a "professional." As a matter of fact, there are a lot of people in the business world who are referred to as "business prostitutes." These are people who have no moral values, no core. They are living for the moment, with no life purpose. They are just out to make a buck for today and get by only for themselves.

A true professional concerns him/herself with their entire team, without losing sight of or violating their own personal goals, expectations, and standards. When you're on the right team, when you're working for the right company, your goals and purposes will align with the group's. This ethical alignment creates win-win situations for all involved.

There are other values you have to evaluate to determine this alignment. A partial list could include:

- **HONESTY**—fairness and straightforwardness of conduct and adherence to the facts or rules

- **PRIDE**—a reasonable or justifiable self-respect. Pride is the delight or elation arising from some act, possession, or relationship.

- **TEAM WORK ETHIC**—the degree to which you and your teams' work habits and efforts positively benefit others.

- **LOYALTY**—an unswerving allegiance to your profession and the people around you.

- **PERSONAL WORK ETHIC**—your habits and efforts pertaining to your profession or focus.

- **INTEGRITY**—a firm adherence to your team's code of moral, artistic, or professional values.

- **TRUST**—an assured, mutual reliance on each other's character, ability, strength, and truthfulness.

- **RELIABILITY**—being dependable to the point where others can count on you.

- **CONSISTENCY**—being marked by harmony, regularity or a steady continuity, free from variation or contradiction.

Make sure your heart is in the right place in these areas. See what other concepts you might add to the list to make it your own. Assume that your life has purpose and direction and that you and your team are always representing your true value orientation.

FAMILY & FRIENDS

When you sit back and reflect on the worth of your life, what do you think about? How much money you've earned? How many touchdowns you scored? How many deals you've closed? I doubt any of these will make the list. What I believe will be high on your list is how you think you did by your family and friends.

As a parent you will likely grade yourself on how you did for your kids. Were you supportive, nurturing, understanding, positive, and committed? Were you an excellent mentor? Did you lead by example? Did you spend enough time doing these things? Did you express unconditional love? Did you put them first and act in their best interest? Did you do the best you could for them in every aspect of life?

Regardless of how successful you are in your career, I have yet to see statistics on a headstone. I doubt you will ever visit a cemetery and see an inscription that says "Johnny Jones 1910-1995 Football Player: led the team in tackles with fifty solos; (1952) Earned $500,000 in his best year." It's the bonds you have made and the relationships you have forged that you will reflect upon when you are in the later stages of the fifth quarter of your life.

YOUR CAREER

Of course careers are important for your self-esteem, respect, earnings, quality of life, and stature in the community. The question is, are you doing or have you done the best you could in all areas of your life? Are you giving 110 percent? Or are you just getting by? Are you that square peg jammed in the round hole, unable to balance your career with your other dreams and passions?

To be completely successful, you must also find the right balance between your career goals and your family values. Today's work force faces a new level of demands and time requirements. The markets are competitive and forever changing. It's a tough world out there. The level of commitment that is required from us all—regardless of our chosen field—can be overwhelming. For most of us, the traditional family dinners are something we only see on television. Several households have two working professionals in them. Sitting down at the same time as a family for a meal just doesn't seem practical today. However, even though a person's career is very important, we all need to keep the proper perspective on what's at the top of the page.

Most organizations respect the people whose value orientation puts their family first and career second. In my career, it was just understood that family time and family events were more important to me than my career. When my son played football on the freshman high school team, it was understood I would leave early on game days so I could cheer him on. The same was true when he was on the varsity team, including away games in distant cities. I left work early, even if I was in an important meeting on Friday afternoon. I was fortunate to be in situations where my choices were almost always respected and accepted.

In my professional development business, there are some clients who insist on holding their classes over the weekend. They don't want to take their people out of the field for too long. We are happy to accommodate these requests, most of the time. Training classes and keynote speaking represent 80 percent of my company's income. However, more than once I had to tell prospects I could not accommodate them on a fall weekend due to my family commitments. I never lost an opportunity because of this. People always understood and were happy to work around familial obligations.

Also, consider these other aspects of your career: Are you making a difference? Is the work you do worthy of your skills and talents? Does it provide you with rewarding and fulfilling opportunities to serve the needs of others? If the answer to these questions is sincerely and passionately yes, then you will inevitably be very successful—provided you are following the principles contained in this book.

By the way, there are many ways you can serve the needs of others besides being a fireman, policeman, doctor, teacher, nurse, lawyer, politician, salesperson, coach. As long as you are providing an ethical product or service, you are serving the needs of others. Just make sure you have a passion for your career and you keep it in perspective with your core values. Only then will you find complete fulfillment within your profession and your life.

FIRE-READY-AIM

Focus makes all of these things possible. Would you set out on a cross-country trip without having a clearly defined destination and purpose in mind for the trip? Of course not. You would most likely know where you want to go, how you are going to get there, and why you're going. You would evaluate all your transportation options, then pick the one that seems most prudent to you. The same should be true as you focus on your life. Too many people just drift through their lives. They don't really know where they want to go, how to get there, or why it even matters. I call this the "Fire, ready, aim" approach.

The "fire, ready, aim" approach makes it almost impossible to hit any target. This tactic is just another version of the making-it-up-as-you-go-along school of thought. A football player would never fire, then stand around, then get ready, and then aim to find someone to hit. If that was their approach, they wouldn't play for long. An opponent who gets ready, aims at their target, and then fires would take them out of the game—fast.

If you ever played football, you already know this. To succeed, you just have to translate the secrets of the game of football into the game of life. However, anyone who applies what they read in this book will be able to get ready, take aim, focus, and hit their bull's eye.

CHANGE SAW

There is one dangerous flipside to the fire-ready-aim way of doing things. It's when you miss seeing the forest because of the trees. As this cartoon clearly points out, some people miss great opportunities because they are either too stubborn to change or else they are so busy running around in circles, they can't see the obvious. Opportunity can come knocking at any time and in many ways.

Don't get so caught up in whatever you might be focusing on that you can't recognize a better way of doing something that would enhance your life or increase your productivity. Obviously, a chainsaw would help the woodsman in this cartoon become more productive. Using a new and improved tool, he could work less and lead an easier life. If he would take the time to explore what the "change saw" could do for him, all kinds of opportunities might present themselves. Hacking away with a dull old axe is too hard and too time-consuming.

If you are not where you want to be and you're considering making some changes, let this picture be your guide. Look for a "change saw" to cut down the dead wood that might be impeding your vision or obstructing your ability to focus.

CHAPTER NINE

IMPROVISING ON A BUSTED PLAY

CREATIVITY

My athletes are willing to follow my advice as long
as it doesn't conflict with their views.
COACH LOU HOLTZ

Everyone has creativity. As a human quality, it is one of our best—the one that elevates us above all the other species on this planet. The word "creativity" means many things to many people. My favorite definition is this one: creativity is the ability to reach beyond conventional limits or traditional wisdom in the pursuit of something new and different.

It benefits us to utilize our creativity every day, regardless of our professional pursuits. Tapping into your creativity **will help you reach your full potential.**

When I was a young'un in school, if the teacher gave me a crayon and a blank piece of paper, I would create the most magical pictures anyone had ever seen—or at least I thought so! For many of us, as we grow up, we seem to lose that spark of spontaneity. However, the good news is that, no matter what age you are, you can always revitalize your creativity! And that is what this chapter is all about.

First above all else, respect your need to create. Your ideas are your future waiting to be born. Do the work necessary to strengthen your belief in your creative abilities and understand the importance of your creative acts.

Creativity refers to much more than just writing a poem or painting a picture. Creativity is all about breaking the chains of the ordinary. My mom used to ask (as only mothers can) things like, "If Billy ran his bike into a wall, would you, too?" Of course, the answer was always no, and the questions made me feel like an idiot. But from my observations consulting around the world, I'm not sure the answer *is* always no. It is astonishing to observe an entire group of people following the same actions of someone else, even when this is not getting the desired results. It's like watching a bunch of cattle, one by one, following the cow in front of them to the slaughterhouse. To get "outside the box," you have to elevate your thinking, dare to be different, and follow your own vision.

THE BOX

If we all followed the same paths, had the same thought processes, and went through the same routines, we would be robots. It is the creative people who make a difference in the world we live in. Every exceptionally successful person has performed at least one creative act on his or her way to fame and fortune.

Football teams utilize creativity all the time. Just look at the playbooks. Teams have plays like the onside kick, the faked punt, the quarterback sneak, the statue of liberty, reverses, and the faked field goal, just to name a few. When outstanding teams put that creativity into action on the field, it's great to watch.

Once, when I was at a college game, I witnessed a great display of creativity. Southern Methodist University's offense came up to the line of scrimmage in the usual way. The quarterback started barking out signals. Apparently, he was ready to run the play. Suddenly, he stopped. He walked a couple of steps to his left. It looked as if he was calling an audible to change the play. But that was the creativity of this moment: just as the quarterback took those few steps to his left, the center surprised the entire defense by snapping the ball directly to the running back. Since all eyes were focused on the quarterback, the defense was caught flat-footed and the offense came away with a very nice gain. Creativity works!

Individual football players demonstrate a fair amount of creativity as well. It's not unusual to see a running back completely shift directions, as if he were making up his own play. Receivers are always changing their routes when the quarterback is scrambling, trying to make something positive happen.

Rick Stroud of the *St. Petersburg Times* recognized this out-of-the-box thinking in Coach Jon Gruden of the Tampa Bay Buccanners.[1] Stroud

1   Stroud, Rick. "Jon Gruden // Extra edge // His creative plays confound opponents." St. Petersburg Times. 24 Jan. 2003. 1X. Tampaby.com. 18 March 2004. <http//:pqasb.pqarchiver.com/sptimes/access/280267551.html?dids=280267551:2802675 5&FMT=FT&FMTA=ABS:FT&type=current&date=Jan=24%2C+2003&author=Rick=St roud&pub=St.+Petersburg+Times&edition=&startpage=1X&desc=Jon+Gruden+%2F%F+

recognized that Jon Gruden's voice was not only in the ears of his quarterback but was always in the heads of the opposing defense as well. Stroud wrote that Gruden's savvy and creative play calling was responsible for the Bucs' appearance in Super Bowl XXXVII, "Time after time ... Gruden has dialed up the right play in the right situation, sometimes to the wonderment of his players." In the same article, quarterback, Brad Johnson, acknowledged Gruden's creativity as well:

> We were playing in Cincinnati earlier in the year, and we had this play-action fake to the tailback and kind of get a combination (route) to the right…And at halftime, [Gruden] said, "Listen, if they come weak side (on a pass rush), be ready to drift in the pocket, roll out to the right a little bit, and buy yourself a little extra time." Son of a gun if he didn't call the play. They come weak and I'm thinking, it's just clicking. I kind of roll out to the right and hit Ken Dilger on a little underneath route and he scores a touchdown.,,, The first time I came over there I said, "Man, that was a great coaching point that you gave me." I told him, "I'm here to learn, give me some more. Feed me, feed me."

Anyone can write the alphabet. But put the letters in the right order and you might win a Pulitzer. The same is true about drawing plays on a chalkboard and knowing when to use them. Gruden not only studies defenses, he spends as much time charting his own tendencies. The Buccaneer's offensive line coach Bill Muir complemented Gruden's creativity as well: "Here's the deal. He thinks outside the box, he's not orthodox ... So some of the things he thinks about, the motion, the movements, he's very creative." Muir goes on to describe a play that totally confused the opponent: "You can watch San Francisco go with the first movement and they're lost.… The pitch went to

Extra+edge+%2F%2F+His+creative+plays+confound+opponents+Series%3A+SUPER+BO
WL+XXXVII%3A+SAN+DIEGO>

the left to Mike Alstott, who practically walked into the end zone." And then Muir summed it up best: "the consensus is Gruden is a great motivator. But offensively, he also is an innovator."

A NEW SHOE

Let's take a look at how well you score when it comes to innovation. When was the last time you got out of the box and did something creative? What is the most creative thing you have ever done? These two questions are the ones I ask when I want to measure how interviewees think. I've done thousands of these interviews. The objective is to investigate a potential employee's entrepreneurial spirit to determine if he or she is willing to try new ideas.

Every organization needs individuals who have different creative viewpoints and the courage to act on their vision. I want to find out if a potential employee can bring something unique to the table. I won't hire anyone who is simply content to follow other cows on their way to the slaughterhouse.

One particular story stands out in my mind. I was once interviewing a man named Scott Johnson. When I asked him, "What is the most creative thing you have ever done in business?" he told me his story.

Scott had developed a unique product—a creative act in itself, and he wanted to sell it to Oracle. Oracle is one of the largest software companies in the world, and Scott knew it would perfectly augment their already robust solution set. However it has, like any large company, multiple levels of management and bureaucracy. It can be tough to get through all these levels when you're trying to sell something to Oracle. After a few meetings with company execs, Scott realized that the only way he'd be able to sell his product to Oracle was to meet with their CEO, Larry Ellison.

Mr. Ellison is not the type of person who sits in his office waiting for the phone to ring, hoping the caller will have something to sell to him. On the contrary, this man is extremely busy. His schedule is always packed. Scott knew that if he was going to get to Oracle's CEO, it would take two ingredients: persistence and creativity.

First, persistence. For ten days running, Scott called Mr. Ellison's office every day, several times a day. Each time he called, the administrative assistant — a.k.a. "the Gate Keeper"—would politely inform him that Mr. Ellison was not available. With all these phone calls, Scott eventually developed a rapport with the Gate Keeper. Gradually, he convinced her to help him get his foot in the door, literally.

Now the creativity. Scott bought a new pair of wing-tipped shoes. He then wrote a note and put it in one of the shoes. Scott sent this shoe-plus-note to the Gate Keeper who agreed to put it on her boss's desk. The note? "Now that I have one shoe in the door, I'll have the other at your office at 7:00 a.m. this Wednesday." Scott showed up at 7:00 a.m. Wednesday morning, wearing the other shoe, ready for his meeting.

Do you think Mr. Ellison was there waiting for Scott at 7:00 a.m.? Absolutely not! As I said before, this CEO was very busy and his time was precious. However, Scott sat there patiently—cooling his heels—and finally got in to see the boss at 10:00 a.m. Mr. Ellison told him he had five minutes. That's all Scott needed. Oracle bought Scott's entire company two weeks later.

Creativity is almost always rewarded and appreciated. Scott had nothing to lose. There was no chance of him selling the company without this meeting. He couldn't even get a phone call returned! At that point he had two choices: A. Walk away defeated. B. Get creative. He made the right call.

COMPLACENCY END ZONE

Descriptive words like average, status quo, mediocre, and ordinary are the brothers and sisters of complacency. What about you? Are you complacent?

Here are some simple questions to find out: Are you learning something new every day? Are you moving forward in your relationships? Your goals? Your life's purpose? Are you being creative?

If you answered no, that's okay—as long as you are willing to do something about it. The only way to avoid complacency and achieve your full potential is to take action. A complacent person will procrastinate in their actions. In the diagram below, you will note a black box with a genie's lamp inside. That black box is the one we need to start thinking outside of. Just like any dark room, the black box is unsettling because you don't know what is inside. What if there is no magic lamp? What if the only thing inside your box is emptiness and darkness? So what? Would you rather find a way out, or just be mediocre your whole life? Would you rather bring moonbeams home in a jar and be better off than you are? Or would you rather just be average?

Achieving your full potential is not a function of circumstance, it is a conscious choice. Conscious choices mean effort, time, and a willingness to change. And change always takes work!

You can't be afraid of entering your black box because that's where your creativity lives. There is a magic genie's lamp inside. It might have been some time since you've seen it, but it's there. You will also find that you have an unlimited number of wishes with this lamp. Forget that old three-wish limitation. This is the twenty-first century! We've upgraded! You get unlimited wishes, enhanced by your actions and creative thinking.

BLACK BOX

Average	Greatness
Ordinary	Fulfillment
Status Quo	Success

COMPLACENCY

Greatness is not a function of circumstance, it is a conscious choice.

TIME OUT

There is no perfect time to be creative. In order to experience your creativity, you will have to become a little more flexible regarding some "priorities." **These are the repetitive activities you do every day in life. The world won't come to an end if you don't clean the dishes,** wash the car, or mow your lawn this very minute. Sometimes these simple tasks can eat your time up and squelch your creativity. Instead of dealing with the mundane, carve out some time to put creativity high on your to-do list today. There are always excuses, reasons and justifications why we can't achieve. Those excuses are the building blocks of complacency. Knock them down.

Take thirty minutes—or even an hour—and do something creative. Dare to break the mold! Turn off the TV! Create! That's how I wrote this book. I usually work about twelve hours a day, six days a week. On top of that, there are four kids and a wife to tend to, a daily exercise regimen, house projects and too many other responsibilities to list. A friend of mine suggested I create the time to write this book by getting up an hour earlier or going to bed an hour later. I was to use that extra hour only on the book. It took some effort, but I created that hour. Actually I ended up creating more than that. I bet you can too.

CREATIVITY-TO-GO

Sometimes ideas need long blocks of time to develop. However, there are other creative steps you can accomplish in short bursts. For those, you need to practice what I call "Creativity-to-Go." While you're sitting in the doctor's waiting room, research magazines. While you're on hold on the phone, sketch ideas for your next venture. Brainstorm with your friends at the gym. Contrary to popular opinion, creativity and real life aren't mutually exclusive. In fact, it's just the opposite. In proper balance, each enhances the other.

Everywhere you go, there are opportunities to think creatively. Next time you walk into a restaurant, observe what you might change to make it better. Think about potential improvements, what you might do differently. Look at magazines ads and ask yourself if they are creative and clever enough. How would you change them? And by the way, after you finish this book, I'd be happy to hear how *you* would have written it to make it to be more purposeful!

CREATIVITY GONE WILD

I really enjoy watching creative plays in a football game. When they work, I cheer at the top of my lungs! I call the coach a genius and the players, heroes.

Once, during a close game against the Naval Academy, Rice University's Coach Hatfield fooled everyone. As I explained in chapter 7, his famous triple option offense does not pass too often. In that offense, a pass is creative. At any rate, this particular game was tied. Both teams were slugging it out on the ground. Rice's offense lined up in the triple option formation with three running backs in the backfield as usual. The quarterback called the play; the fullback went through the line, and the ball was pulled. The quarterback started to sprint around the end as if to run the traditional option. Suddenly, he pulled up and threw a forty-yard pass—not to a wide receiver, but to the fullback! Coach Hatfield had put in a fullback streak! At first glance you might think: a fullback streak? Fullbacks don't run forty-yard streaks. In this case, however, Rob was the fullback. He happened to be one of the fastest players Rice had. There were very few linebackers who could keep up with him. Sure enough, Coach Hatfield's call and Rob's execution gave the Owls a game-winning touchdown. Once again, creativity was rewarded.

Okay football fans: What happens when you see your favorite team employ a creative play and the coach's call backfires? Have you seen a team run the reserves play only to lose twelve yards? Or run a fake punt on fourth down and not convert? Or worse, the easy chip-shot field goal, but the team fakes it and comes away with no points? The coaches and players involved go from the penthouse of genius to the outhouse of stupidity. Heaven forbid running multiple creative plays that don't work. In less than a New York minute, the fans will be calling for a new coach.

Did you ever stop to think that your own mindset could be preventing you from exercising your creativity? Are you fearful that your creative idea might not work? Well? So what! There are no fans to boo you, no media writing bad reviews like. "Today Bob sent a telegram to his biggest prospect in a desperate move to get his attention. What a boneheaded move! It completely backfired! The prospect told this reporter "that Bob is a moron! Too bad Bob didn't just follow conventional wisdom. If he had, maybe—just maybe—he could have sold something."

How many times has your self-doubt collided with your nerves and refused to let your creativity move forward? Just as a coach's creative calls or trick plays will not always be successful, your creative ideas and follow-through will not always net you the results you'd like. Worst outcome: You might learn something by trying and failing. Best outcome: Your creativity gets the desired results. One sure thing you can count on: if you don't try, you'll never know. And you will slowly fall into the complacency zone.

In football the trick plays that backfire really can bring widespread ridicule to the coach or players. In the world outside of football, well-conceived and creative plans or actions are typically looked upon favorably, regardless of the outcome. I've polled hundreds of people and not found one who recalled a single time their creative actions were criticized or had negative results.

FEED YOUR CREATIVE MIND

There's little joy in being ordinary. Why bother being like everyone else? This doesn't mean you should go out and get body-pierced or tattooed from head to toe with some wild design. No. That's definitely not what I am referring to. I am talking about your productive creativity. How do you reach that? And utilize it?

The first step is to become conscious and active in a creative way. We've already discussed how to be creative during big blocks of time or on the go. Now let's run down this lane a little further.

First, start a "creativity file." It's easy. When you see an ad, a magazine title for an article, or some image that strikes you as creative, cut it out, print it out, and stick in it your file. You can use other peoples' ideas and images to kick-start your own creativity. You're not going to copy what they've done, but you can certainly utilize their inspiration.

CREATIVITY NOT REALIZED

Another effective approach is to start a creative journal. Write down your random thoughts in a notebook. It doesn't matter what they are. It does matter that you act on these ideas.

I had an idea two decades ago about selling season tickets for out-of-town football games. The idea was that fans who were loyal to teams outside of their game-viewing area would pay to watch them on TV. I know that when I moved from Cincinnati to Georgia, I would have loved to watch the Bengal's play on Sundays. But Bengal games were nowhere to be found in Atlanta. Since every NFL game is broadcast and televised somewhere, why not sell cable TV packages to all the people who have moved yet still want to follow their favorite teams? Sounds good doesn't it? It was a solid, creative idea. Today it's called *Direct NFL Sunday Ticket*. Guess how much I earned off my creative idea? Zero. It's great to have a journal of creative ideas, but ideas only pay off when you act on them.

Creativity breeds fresh new thoughts. It's the action and execution of these new thoughts that breed success. As I stated earlier, all businesses started with an individual's entrepreneurial creative spirit. Regardless of the current size of the organization—IBM, AT&T, Coke—they all started with a single creative idea put into action. Interview the most successful person you know. Ask him or her if he or she regularly acts on their own creativity. The answer will be a resounding yes!

Football coaches and players will also agree. Successful people know the value of employing creativity and action. They know that creative and well-executed ideas breed success.

CHAPTER TEN

BECOMING A GAMER

COURAGE & CHARACTER

You can learn more character on the two-yard line
than you can anywhere in life.

PAUL DIETZEL

FORMER ARMY COACH

Courage is the mental or moral strength to venture, persevere, and withstand real or perceived danger. It takes a high level of courage to participate and compete in any sport; however, football provides the supreme test.

Each time football players put on their pads, they are expected to go out and give 100 percent, no matter the risk. Imagine this: you are 5' 11" and weigh two hundred pounds. For one reason or another, in today's game you're pitted against a guy who is six-foot eight-inches and weighs 350 pounds.

In football, these mismatches happen all the time. They can scare the daylights out of you! Even if you're big and tall, it's pretty frightening to have a fired up, three-hundred-pound hulk bearing down on you, trying his best to knock you into next week. Chicago Bears' Hall of Fame Linebacker Dick Butkus was once quoted as saying, "I wouldn't ever set out to hurt anybody deliberately, unless it was important—like a league game or something." Thanks, Dick. With that in mind, it's easy to see how one can get hurt in this game!

Fact is, in almost any high-level football game, you will see a player with his hand or arm so heavily padded, you'd think he had a club underneath. In reality, it's a broken hand, arm, or wrist. It makes no sense to risk further injury, but there they are, out there playing the game. Football provides this test of courage to all who play. In my opinion, no other sport incorporates this intensity.

I often work with people who need to be able to muster up more courage in the business world. They might be afraid to call on a senior executive in an attempt to secure their business. Or they are scared to share their true feelings about a situation. Or they fear change. Or whatever. The list is endless. We all deal with our own fears. People who have played the game of football understand what it means to face and conquer their fears. You can too.

MEET THE RHINO

Kelly Rhino springs from a couple of generations of football players. His grandfather was an All-American at Georgia Tech. His father, Randy, was also an All-American football player at Tech. Now, the Rhinos are not big men. Kelly was definitely size-challenged. He was all of about five-foot seven-inches and weighed 170 pounds soaking wet. In high school, he played for a dominant football team. His was the kind of team where everyone looks like they are already in college. Their game scores were so lopsided, the coaches would send in the benchwarmers after halftime, just to show good sportsmanship. It was very typical each week to see several three hundred-pound players lined up against Kelly's high school team.

One of the most amazing things about Kelly was that he played fullback! Think about this kid's courage: he faced three hundred-pound defensive tackles, play after play. Kelly played like it didn't even bother him. Every play, he just put his head down and did his best to move the mountain of human flesh opposing him. The funny thing is, he won the battle more often than not! You couldn't help but shake your head when you saw Rhino knock some guy off his feet—especially when that opponent was twice his size. It was really stunning. And every once in a while—after butting heads with Kelly—the larger player would hobble off the field in search of the medical trainer.

I had the pleasure of watching Kelly play for years. I never saw him get hurt, quit on a play, or cower away from what appeared to be an impossible assignment.

In the family tradition, Kelly was awarded a full athletic scholarship to Georgia Tech. This five-foot-nothing, 170-pound athlete was about to face big-time college football.

The people who watched Kelly play in high school were not surprised to hear that he earned a starting position as punt returner for Georgia Tech. In order to play this position, one has to have exceptional courage. The opposing team kicks the ball to a single player, the punt returner. As the ball is coming towards the punt returner, eleven defensive players are simultaneously rushing down the field with the intent to knock the dog out of him! More times than not, just as the punt returner is about to catch the ball, there are one or two opposing players within a few steps of him. Keep in mind, these defenders are at their top speed, having just sprinted for forty yards. With that kind of momentum, it is no surprise that punt returners take some of the hardest hits in football.

Kelly Rhino not only handled his responsibilities with courage, he went on to earn All Atlantic Coast Conference honors for his play! Last I heard, Kelly was enyoying a career as a professional player in the Canadian Football league. This is just one example of how courage and the will to succeed can carry you as far as you dream.

HERMINATION

It's amazing what the human body can do when another bigger human body is chasing it. I thought Kelly had retired the trophy for the most courage—until I met Kyle Herm. Kyle was about the same size as Kelly, five-foot-seven-inches, and 170 pounds. I didn't have the privilege of watching Kyle through high school, but he was someone special, even then.

It was totally remarkable to watch Kyle at his size play at quarterback *for a running team*. Kyle was the starting quarterback for the Fighting Owls of Rice University. As I've said in earlier chapters, Rice specializes in the triple option offense. What this means is they do not pass the ball much. More often than not, they run it. The quarterback has one of three options to run the ball. In most offensive schemes, when the quarterback runs the ball it means that something has gone wrong. In the triple-option playbook, about half the plays are deliberately designed for the quarterback to run the ball. Kyle Herm would run around the end or up the middle (up the middle is also called between-the-tackles). This means there was probably somewhere close to 1,600 pounds of beef that he was running in between or into. There was a huge nose man, two tackles and two or three linebackers whose only job was to crush the guy with the ball. And Kyle weighed about 170 pounds! Yet, I never saw him cower away from anyone even once. He frequently had the chance to take the ball out of bounds, but he rarely did. Instead, he would take on two or three defensive players just to get that extra yard. Kyle did get hurt more than once, but that didn't faze him. He even played in a game with broken ribs. He became the first player in Rice's history to both rush and pass for two thousand yards in a career. Kyle Herm and Kelly Rhino share the same type of courage and character, as do so many football players.

When you read this, stop to think for a moment about how many times fear has prevented you from taking action in your life. Whether it was asking someone out on a date, requesting a raise, switching jobs, or pursuing your creative passion, fear can totally paralyze a person. Most of the time, these fears don't come about because of immediate life-threatening circumstances. They're usually brought about by things that, when looked upon in retrospect, are comparatively trivial. However, we get so worked up in our minds, these fears seem justifiable and insurmountable.

It is at these moments that we find ourselves at a crossroads with two paths clearly in sight. One path tells us to face our fears, to move forward with courage. The other path tells us not to risk it, to stay where we are. What most of us do when confronted with such a choice is to weigh the risks and assess the possible outcomes.

Football players can usually recall a time when they faced a threatening situation on the playing field and overcame their fears. Cincinnati Bengals linebacker Gary Burley is quoted as saying, "Tackling running back, Earl Campbell is like standing in the middle of Interstate 75, dodging the cars and trying to tackle the biggest truck out there." I'm sure Kelly Rhino felt the same way in reverse.

When Kelly or Kyle ask for a raise at some point in their careers, it's very likely that their boss won't weigh three hundred or more pounds. It's also very likely that Mr. Boss Guy won't come across the desk and pound them into the carpet. If either Kelly or Kyle has to give a speech to their companies, it's very improbable that there would be eleven adrenalin-crazed warriors rushing towards them with the intent to put them in the hospital. But this is exactly what happened on the field, when they were playing football. They not only survived it, they learned from it and thrived on it!

By the way, did you know that—statistically—public speaking ranks ahead of dying as people's number one fear?

The point is that fear comes in all shapes and sizes and is almost always masked as something else. I had a teammate on my high school football team who happened to be the fastest young man in the school. On his first day, he came out to practice wearing his track spikes. Of course you can't wear track spikes to play football: the whole team would have puncture wounds. When the coaches told he couldn't wear the spikes, he quit. Of course, some of us wanted him to wear them for just one play so *he* could learn about courage. But, no such luck.

THE HUMMER

Recall my sons wake-up call and the words that became his motto: "Those who fail to prepare, prepare to fail." After that tough experience, Rob became extremely focused on achieving his goal to play Division I college football. From that point forward, he began working hard—almost too hard. He typically spent an hour and a half running and then another hour and a half in the gym. This resulted in a lot of muscle and incredible speed. In the Georgia State Football Combine (a yearly event where coaches objectively test players from around the state), he ran the forty-yard dash in 4.38 seconds! Even more impressive is he weighed over two hundred pounds! He was the fastest player at that weight in the entire state. And it was pretty hair-raising to see that much weight coming at you that fast. Without question, Rob was in the best shape of his life. He had built his body up to bench-press almost four hundred pounds. There was not enough weight in the gym for him to max out when he was leg pressing. It looked like Rob was ready to make his mark. It looked like he would break all records during his final year in high school.

After the team was into ten days of summer practice, I ran into the coach. I asked how Rob was doing. The coach said they couldn't believe it when Rob first took off his shirt. It was obvious how hard he had been working. Then the coach said, "That's all great. But we really need to do something about his aerobic conditioning. He goes two plays and has to stop." That made no sense to me. I told the coach how Rob had been running his butt off all summer. How could he possibly be out of shape? I thought maybe Rob had mono or something, but I knew he wasn't out of shape. I also knew that if Rob didn't have a good senior season, his college athletic aspirations would vanish forever.

We arranged for Rob to see a doctor. After several tests they determined that Rob did not have mono. It was worse; he had asthma. How could a perfectly healthy teenage athlete suddenly develop asthma? Well, as we soon found out there is an athletically induced asthma. Basically, every time a player gets over-excited or over-heated, the asthma flares up. Imagine what this means to a football player, especially one who runs the ball. Rob got some medicine that helped a little; however, it did not alleviate his shortness of breath and quick fatigue.

At this point, it would have been easy for Rob to quit playing football. It also would have been understandable. How could he possibly go out on the playing field, day after day, with an anvil sitting on his chest? In Rob's case, he showed a lot of courage. He tried to act like nothing was wrong. He didn't quit. He wouldn't come out of a game unless he was about to go unconscious. Rob showed a different kind of courage than Kelly and Kyle, and it was just as impressive, if not more so.

You might be thinking "That's all very nice. But *I'm* not playing in a game that requires this level of courage everyday. How does any of this relate to me?" Guess what. You are playing a game that requires even *more* courage.

We all have decision points in our lives. At each one of these points, we can choose to fight courageously or not. Granted, no huge "office linebacker" is likely to bowl you over if you show up a little late for work, or miss an assignment, or perform your job poorly. Still, every day is Game Day out in the working world, so the need for courage *does* apply to you. In spades!

It takes a lot of courage to learn new things, to explore new opportunities and to take calculated risks. The most successful people in the world often started with nothing but a dream. These captains of industry turned out to be successful beyond imagination. But they weren't *always* on top of the heap. It took courage for them to follow their dreams.

Ted Tuner's story is well documented. The short version is that he started with a bankrupt billboard company his father left him. He turned it around and went on to become one of the richest people in the country. In the beginning of his career, Mr. Turner faced the choice of whether to sell the company's few remaining billboards or to try to turn the company around.

He committed to turning the company around. Further, he had the courage to stick with his choice until he succeeded. We make business decisions every day that involve some level of courage.

Most people reach a point and convince themselves, "This is as far as I go. This is as good as it gets." Whether it's their relationships, their jobs, careers, earnings, you name it, this complacency limits their chance for success. Their fear paralyzes them. Or they lack enough courage to risk venturing into the unknown. Of course the unknown can be a scary place. It takes courage to overcome your fear and achieve your full potential.

Ask yourself, "Am I in a situation that's not great, but not bad enough to risk a change? Am I doing better than most, but am I less well-off than others? Am I just putting my time in at the office, just getting by with a mediocre level of success?" Have you decided not to upset the applecart because your goals were too lofty anyway? Have you convinced yourself it's all "good enough"? If you answered yes to any of the above, you have a serious case of complacency.

But complacency doesn't have to be fatal. And it definitely doesn't have to be permanent. If you are not where you want to be in any area of your life, ask yourself this one question: What's the worst thing that could happen if you took a risk to reach for where you'd like to be?

Then ask yourself this question: What is the best that could happen? And, finally: What are you doing every day to make sure the best is going to happen?

There's a saying: You're either green and growing or ripe and dying. So, all you have to do to change for the better is to get growing!

My biggest fear is the "what if" question. What if I had done this, or tried that, or called on this person, or taken that job? We should all be *less* afraid of failing and *more* afraid of *not trying*. If you try something new and you fail, you should be able to live with that. Fact is, if you are truly committed to what you are trying to achieve, you won't fail. Think of the things you have really wanted and actually gotten in your lifetime. Not the nice-to-haves, but the must-haves. With courage and commitment, they became yours. There is an age-old saying: "If you can conceive it, you can achieve it." You have to have the courage to do both.

I've met too many people who have told me all the things they wanted to do—or were going to do—but just never got around to it. Their reason for not doing it is that "they ran out of time," or some other excuse. There are always excuses for what we do not achieve. Most of them are "totally understandable." It's how we justify the "why's" and "cant's."

Rob had all kinds of reasons why it would have been okay not to reach his goal of a Division I football scholarship. He would have been totally justified to give up. He had asthma. *He couldn't breathe right!* But he didn't quit. He'd chosen his true path. He was a football player. And he had the courage it took to stay on that path.

You have the potential to exhibit that same kind of courage. At the end of the day, the path you pursue is up to you.

I'm Okay, You're not Okay

In my career, I was usually an executive. As President or Vice President, I had several people working under me. Each environment required consistent, predictable results. That mandate was handed down throughout the staff. Unfortunately, not everyone could achieve the level of results that were required. Those who couldn't, I had to let go. Without exception, their internal and external justification for their termination was that it was *not their fault.* It was the *always* the company, the market, the management, or a host of other issues. Good-sounding excuses, but they were just not true.

Ask a salesperson how they were able to secure that new account or nail that large sale. The answer you will hear 99.9 percent of the time is correct: superior salesmanship. They will likely go on to share their masterful strategy. They will describe in detail the relationships they built with the decision-maker and the creativity they applied while setting traps for the competition. Most sales people will stop just short of pounding their chests.

Now ask the exact same person why they lost an opportunity or why they haven't been achieving the required results. I will fall on the floor the first time I hear, "I wasn't good enough"; "I got sloppy"; "I skipped steps"; "I got out-sold." Instead, they'll typically say it was the manager's fault, the tight market, the over-priced product, the lack of leads, or a host of other excuses. The fact is if they had the courage to admit their mistakes, they would continue to learn new methods of selling. They would discover more about the market. More important, they would overcome their complacency. Then they *could* beat their chests in victory.

It took courage for me to write this book. Thoughts would creep in to interrupt me. "What if people don't like this book? What if everyone disagrees with my ideas? What if they don't understand the secret of football? What if no one buys my book? What if I look like a fool?" And on and on and on. As intimidated as I was, I just kept writing. Personally, I would rather face the music than not offer the gift of understanding. For me, the potential rewards far outweigh the risks.

The same complacent attitude that holds individuals back can impact a company's success and growth as well. How many times have you heard, "If it's not broke, why fix it?" Aging product lines, lack of an investment in people and products, the lack of vision to the changing needs in the marketplace are death sentences to a company's growth and prosperity.

Someone at McDonald's showed some real courage when they proposed offering a breakfast menu. What if no one came to McDonalds for breakfast?

McDonalds is not known for breakfast. There are many other restaurants that offer breakfast. I can almost hear the typically risk-averse corporate executives voicing all the reasons why this new idea wouldn't work. But it did.

Arthur Blank showed real courage when he co-founded Home Depot in 1978. Back then, there was a hardware store on just about every corner. Think of what the nay-sayers must have said to Mr. Blank. The nay-sayers are our friends, our family, and the little voices inside our heads telling us why something can't be done. They point out the impending doom that will fall on us if we pursue our dreams. Obviously, Arthur Blank had the courage to ignore them.

The same goes for self-made millionaires. They make their fortunes, can lose it at some point, and then make it all back again, plus more. At first glance, that makes no sense. How can a person dedicate himself to making millions of dollars, do all the work necessary to achieve that goal…and then lose it? When you dig a little deeper, it makes perfect sense. Self-made millionaires take healthy risks and work very hard. They continually improve themselves, extend their reach, and apply the risk and reward formula. If they come up empty—or even worse, find themselves in serious financial straits—they spring right back up again. You'd think they might be depressed or discouraged—that they'd find reasons to quit. Of course, any of these attitudes would be understandable. But if that were their make-up, they wouldn't have achieved their success in the first place. If they take a risk that somehow doesn't pay off, they apply the same principles of success and courage to take the next calculated risk to earn it all back again.

COURAGE EXEMPLIFIED

One of the most courageous stories I know is about a college football player named Neil Parry. Like so many other high school athletes, he dreamed of playing Division I college football. After a great high-school career, he realized that dream. He was offered a full athletic scholarship to San Jose State. He worked his way into the starting lineup and made a measurable contribution to the team's success. Then, in a game against the University of Texas, he was hurt, suffering a severe compound fracture to his leg. Even though he received excellent medical treatment, his leg got infected. Then it got worse. Finally, Parry had to have his leg amputated. This had to be devastating to Neil, to his family, his friends, and his teammates. However, this young man had learned the secret of football. Instead of giving up, he made a vow to play football again.

After twenty-five operations, fifteen prosthetic legs and countless hours of rehab, Neil made it back onto the field as the first non-kicker to suit up for NCAA football with a prosthetic limb.

Neil understood courage and sacrifice. If he applies just a fraction of the other characteristics of success he learned from playing football, his future will be extremely bright. He had the courage not to quit, the courage not to sit around and feel sorry for himself. He had the courage to really believe it was possible to play football again. That kind of courage can be an inspiration to us all.

Passive Acceptance

Passive acceptance is when a person accepts a given circumstance. He or she feels there is nothing they can do to change, impact, or overcome the situation. Neil's leg, Rob's asthma, and Kyle and Kelly's stature were all very difficult circumstances to have and still excel in the game of football. Each of these courageous young men could have just passively "accepted their fate."

Instead, they courageously pursued their goals and dreams. By their actions, they all revealed their true character.

CHARACTER

The word character is derived from words that mean, "engraved," and "inscribed." This derivation implies something important: our character is written, inscribed and engraved in and on everything we do. Character guides our thoughts, feelings, and actions. In the world of sports, football gives each player countless opportunities to reveal their character. The players' actions on the field read like an open book.

Football teaches players how to win and lose, the importance of rules, teamwork, how to deal with controversy, how to learn from disappointment and—perhaps most importantly—how to accept and appreciate good coaching, even if you might not initially agree with some of the orders.

After all, a coach really is a teacher. The good ones contribute to forming character. They great ones teach lessons that transcend the game. We've all witnessed a young football player with exceptional skills who gets pulled out of the game for one reason or another. Sometimes a meltdown follows: the player slams down his helmet, yells, and throws a fit. On most teams this kind of behavior is not tolerated. Of course, no true competitor ever wants to leave a game. However, an immature reaction to the coach's decision might keep them out of the game even longer.

Then there is the player who is asked to move to a different position or perform a duty they might not want to. In this case there are three basic responses:

A. Protest and refuse to do what is being asked of you.

B. Take on new or additional responsibility with the intention of not performing at the highest level possible

C. Take on a new position or more responsibilities with the sincere intention of doing your absolute best.

The only other reasonable response would be to share your feelings about what is being asked of you and to discuss why you are feeling the way you do. After that discussion—or series of discussions—you will still have to choose from *A*, *B* or *C*. Only *C* shows real character.

Rob had to make this choice at a critical moment in his football career. In his first ten years of playing football, Rob had been a tailback. He was used to running the ball, scoring lots of touchdowns and receiving a great deal of recognition from the teams he played on. When Rob began his sophomore season in high school, the coach wanted Rob to switch his position.

This might not seem like a big deal, but it was to Rob. As you know, he had aspirations of playing Division I college football and winning a scholarship. As such, his sophomore year was very important. Rob wanted to play on the varsity squad so as to attract the attention of college scouts early. Once the scouts become aware of a player as a sophomore, they tend to follow his junior and senior campaigns. Since Rob had been playing football for ten years as a tailback, switching to a new position could have been detrimental to achieving his goal.

He accepted the change like a man. He trusted that the coaches saw something in him that would make the change a good idea, for both Rob and the team. So, at that point in his high-school football career, Rob graciously moved to the fullback position.

As a fullback, he got to carry the ball once in a while, but his main responsibility was to block for the tailback and quarterback. That meant less public recognition, fewer touchdowns, less glory and—most important—that Rob had to learn how to play an entirely new position. Fullbacks are usually much larger than he was at this point, so I also questioned the change. But I remained silent. I decided to let Rob handle it however he chose. I knew this was an opportunity for him to test his character.

Remember the *A*, *B*, and *C* above? Rob chose *C*. He decided to give 100 percent. He performed his new role/position the best he could.

By displaying outstanding character, Rob was able to become one of the best fullbacks to ever play for his high school team. He was also recognized as one of the best senior fullbacks in the state. It was ironic how the change to fullback and Rob's attitude played out. Making the right decision led to his dreams coming true.

When Rob was a senior, Baylor University was initially very interested in offering him a scholarship. After watching lots of film of his play, Baylor later decided not to make an offer to Rob. After so much attention and so many conversations, I was very curious why they decided not to move forward. The school's coach told me that they were really in search of a tailback. They already had several players at the fullback position. After watching how Rob played, he determined he was a great fullback but was not a tailback.

The decision to accept the change to fullback opened the door to an offer from a more prestigious university. Obviously, the high school coach knew exactly what he was doing when he switched Rob's position. Rob showed character in accepting this change, and it resulted in even greater success for him. If he keeps this same character and applies it outside of football, he should move on to great things in his life.

However, sadly, for every story like Rob's, there are hundreds more just like it where the person chooses to react in a different way, like a boy named Bill Royal.

Football doesn't build character. It eliminates the weak ones.

COACH DARREL

Bill was also a star high school football player. He was captain of the team and one of the best linebackers in the state. One day the coach told Bill that the team needed him to play both ways, on offense and defense. When the coach asked Bill to play offensive guard, Bill thought to himself, "No way!" Not only would Bill get fatigued and risk injury by playing both ways, there was no glory whatsoever in the guard position. An offensive guard is a lineman with the sole job of blocking the defensive players.

Bill took choice *B*. He accepted the additional responsibilities, but every time the coach put him in at guard, Bill basically just lay down and blocked no one. He always had a reason why he hadn't made the block. Some of the reasons were valid, but it was easy to see that Bill just didn't want the job. He was all about himself and not about the team. Bill's poor blocking continued until the coach finally had to replace him at the guard position with another player.

Bill's reward was to be moved back to linebacker position, full time. So, did Bill get what he wanted? Nope. "What goes 'round, comes 'round." His selfish attitude and lack of character came back to bite him. At the end of the season, the college scouts visited Bill's coaches to inquire about his skills, attitude, and character. Bill's high school coaches were not supportive. They couldn't and wouldn't recommend that any college take a chance on him.

Even though Bill finished the season as one of the top defensive players in the state, he did not receive a single scholarship offer. His playing days were over. His total self-involvement worked counter to everything he hoped to gain. Bill learned a hard lesson at the age of eighteen.

Every one of us faces situations that test our character daily. And I'm not referring here to natural disasters or life-changing events. It's the day-to-day tests that truly say something about our character. These are the ones that we will judge our lives by when we are old, sitting on the porch, and reflecting on the paths we chose.

There will be times when someone will ask something of you. There will be other times when you find yourself in a character-testing situation. If you have faith that these events happen for a reason, you will use the opportunity to build your character. If you follow this path, you will probably be able to maintain a positive outlook throughout your life, regardless of the circumstances. Without a doubt, you will be asked to perform duties you might not want to do and put in situations you'd prefer didn't exist. You might be asked to move your family across country for additional job responsibilities. You might be given an assignment you are not sure you can do. Circumstances such as these force you to reach inside yourself and determine which path to take.

Someone once told me they thought a person's character is also tested and measured when they have a choice to do something that they know is wrong and the likelihood that they would get caught is slim. It's at this point they have to choose their path. The opposite can be true as well; that is, when someone does something commendable and does not care if anyone else knows about it.

SLICE OF PIZZA—SLICE OF LIFE.

My friend, an ex-football player named Jimmy, faced just such a situation. He had a friend named Ralph who opened a pizza franchise with a buddy of his named Tom. Ralph and Tom wanted a third partner to help with the capital outlay needed to launch the business. Ralph asked Jimmy to come aboard. The opportunity seemed very solid, and the plan looked great, even though Jimmy didn't quite trust Tom. But since the larger, better-known chains of pizza stores were earning an estimated $40,000 in a weekend, Jimmy thought it was a sound investment.

With Ralph's recommendation, Jimmy was in. He made it very clear from the get-go to his two new business partners that he would not have time to personally run the business. His role was to invest his share of the money and offer advice from the sidelines. The business grew until the partnership had four stores up and running.

After twenty-four months in operation, the pizza stores were just about breaking even, even though it had been a very rocky two years. At that time, Jimmy accepted a promotion in the company he worked for. This meant Jimmy had to move halfway across the country. Tom continued to run the day-to-day operations, and Ralph remained involved on a limited basis.

One night, one of the pizza delivery drivers was killed in a car accident while delivering a pizza. This was a terrible situation for everyone involved. It was the final straw in a business that had been a financial roller-coaster. After the accident, the business shut down. Jimmy, Ralph, and Tom lost their investments. The main reason the company failed was that Tom had grossly mismanaged the business. Jimmy learned the valuable lesson of not putting your fate in someone else's hands. As you can imagine, he was not happy with this.

About a year later, Jimmy received a message from Ralph that he needed to talk to him about the pizza company. Jimmy thought this was strange since they had shut the company down. He called Ralph to see what was up. The conversation went something like this: "Jimmy I know I recommended Tom, and I know you really didn't trust him. We have a situation we have to deal with. Basically, Tom did not pay any payroll taxes. We owe the IRS $30,000. I would understand it if you don't want to kick in your $10,000. I got you into this deal, and you've already lost enough. However if you can't or you won't, I will end up having to pay $20,000." That offer alone said something about Ralph's character. What would you do? You live several states away, and you had warned Ralph many times about Tom's incompetence. You questioned his trustworthiness, and you are not legally bound to pay $10,000. Keep in mind, this call came with no warning. There are really only two choices: put a check in the mail the next day, or tell him you aren't paying because you told him so, it wasn't your fault, and you've already lost enough money.

Jimmy had learned many lessons on the football field and had developed great character traits. Being human, Jimmy did take the opportunity to say "I told you so," but he also sent a check the next day. How would you have done on this test of character?

The result was that Jimmy and Ralph remained life-long friends. They later did several lucrative business deals together. Ralph had an unwavering trust in Jimmy. He appreciated Jimmy's character. When he had attractive financial opportunities in the future, he offered them to Jimmy. Why? Because Jimmy had shown himself to be a stand-up guy.

I believe a person's character can change and evolve throughout the years, but the core is formed early in life. We all can take personal pride by having and displaying excellent character traits. Your character is something that is revealed in almost everything you do, even in the tiny moments.

It's All About Team

I remember one such moment with Rob. Rob came from a very winning football program in high school. His team never lost a regular season game the entire time he was playing. As a matter of fact, all of Rob's football teams were winners. In a career that spanned eleven years, Rob experienced only about a half dozen losses. Rob went off to college and won a starting role as an eighteen-year-old freshman. At this university, it had been ten years since a true freshman had started in as a fullback. Most freshmen college players are "red-shirted." This means that, for their first year, they are on the team, practice with the team, go to all team meetings, but do not dress or play in the games. This gives freshmen time to grow, mature, learn the speed of the college game, and the system they will be playing in.

Freshmen have a lot to deal with when they go to college. For most freshmen, it's their first time away from home. They are in strange and unfamiliar surroundings. Their scholastic workload is challenging. Even if they are red-shirted, they still have a demanding football schedule and an almost overwhelming commitment to adhere to. It is very rare that true freshmen earn a starting position on Division I college football teams. Rob was the exception.

The first game he played in was against the cross-town rivals, Houston Cougars. Traditionally, it was a highly anticipated game. It was also one of best-attended games of the season. Rob not only started, he scored his team's first touchdown! The game went back and forth. It ended up in tie, which forced the game into overtime. In college overtime situations, each team gets the ball on the twenty-five-yard line. The team that doesn't score or scores the least amount of points loses the game. The opposing team ran several running plays on their effort to score. Their drive stalled, forcing a field-goal attempt. The kick was good and they went ahead by three points. This meant that the Fighting Owls had to score a touchdown to win or at least a field goal to send the game into another overtime. If neither happened, they would lose.

On the first play in overtime, the coaches called a pass play to Rob. He caught it and took it down to the eight-yard line. The very next play was a pass into the end-zone. There was a pass-interference penalty on the defense so Rice got the ball on the one-yard line. They had four tries to cross the goal line to win the game. The next play was a handoff to Rob up the middle for no gain. The next play was a quarterback sneak, again for no gain. The third play was another handoff to Rob. He appeared to score, but the referee said no.

This left the team in a dicey situation. They hadn't been able to score on the previous three downs. Still needing only one yard, the choices were to kick a field goal and force another overtime, or go for the touchdown and risk the game. What play would you call?

After a brief timeout, the coaches decided to go for the touchdown. They called on "#41," their freshman fullback, to carry the load. Rob didn't disappoint. He took it in for the touchdown! Forty thousand fans rushed out onto the field. Fireworks went off in the end zone. Rob's teammates rushed to meet him on the field. If that wasn't enough, as soon as Rob left the field, ESPN, Fox Sports, and the local news all wanted interviews with the star of the game. Not a bad experience for your first game out of high school.

But what does the story have to do with building character? As the story continues, the rest of the season did not go nearly as well for the team. They lost the next few games, even though Rob continued to excel. On the away games, it was standard practice for the players to go into the locker room after the game. They showered, changed out of their uniforms, and then visited with their family and friends before jumping on the team bus, heading to the airport. On one particular Saturday, Rob had played a very solid game, but the team had experienced another disappointing loss. When Rob came out of the locker room, I was there to greet him as usual. I praised his outstanding effort and performance.

This time, he was visibly upset. I couldn't figure out why. Suddenly, my big, tough football-playing son had a tear in his eye! I was totally taken aback by his emotional feelings since Rob rarely expressed anything but positive emotions about anything! He pulled himself together and told me the reason he was feeling so emotional: his team was not winning. It wasn't Rob's fault that the team lost that day. He had played a great game. But he said that his individual stats weren't what mattered. The only thing that really mattered to him was that the *team* win. He was putting the team before his own needs, glory, or gain.

The pride I already felt for my son grew a little deeper. Right then and there, I knew my son possessed the special character traits that would serve him well in the fifth quarter of his life.

CHAPTER ELEVEN

HOLDING THE LINE

MENTAL TOUGHNESS

Toughness is in the soul and spirit, not in muscles.

ALEX KARRAS

ROCK ON

In this chapter, you will see the word "mettle" frequently. And while it may sound the same as "metal," it doesn't refer to any class of physical elements, nor does it describe the traditional head-banging style of rock music. When someone refers to "testing your mettle," they are speaking about your mental toughness. It is the will to persevere, regardless of obstacles. You can measure its strength by how well a person holds true to their objective, even in a pressure-laden situation.

Mettle can bend but it shouldn't break. It is the backbone that an individual or a team demonstrates in the face of adversity.

I have often said, "Never grow a wishbone where a backbone ought to be." Individuals and teams with strong mettle don't wish or wait for things to happen. Instead, they thrive on pressure and use it to take their game up a notch. Usually, every game has two scenarios that provide the test of one's mettle.

The first scenario is when the game is on the line. These are the pressure situations that we all face at times in our lives. Simply surviving a situation or the inevitable mistakes we sometimes make will not provide us the opportunity to test or strengthen our mettle.

Your mettle is tested when your mental toughness is challenged. It is strengthened when you spring back from a failure and demonstrate your determination and will to succeed.

The second scenario is when you have been defeated. You are so far behind, your inclination is to put your tail between your legs and shuffle off the field in your own walk of shame. Your plans have been so thoroughly destroyed that all you really want to do is pack up your bags and go home. You are mentally (and sometimes physically) hurting and you truly want to give up.

Have you ever seen a football team get behind by so many points that they just lay down and run the clock out? There is no "slaughter rule" in football. A slaughter rule is when one team gets so far ahead of the other, the losing team cannot possibly win. So it is deemed a slaughter and the game is called off at that point. There is no slaughter rule in life either!

My wife and I were at one of these football games. One team was up 49 – 7 in the third quarter. It was getting cold. My wife wanted to leave. In this case, I understood why she thought the game was over. It was. However, the losing team did not give up. They insisted on running out of bounds to stop the clock, executing the two-minute drill, shuttling different players in out of the game and using their timeouts as best they could. My wife said, "Why are they dragging this game out? They have no chance to win." She was probably right. I doubt there have been many situations where a team made up a forty-two-point deficit in one-and-a-half quarters. That didn't matter though. The team that was behind had incredible mental toughness. I did not witness one player give up or quit. They were all out there, still trying their absolute best to make something positive happen. In the best case, they might come back and win the game. In the worst case, they could learn a lot of lessons they would build on for the next game. And yes, they did go on to lose, but they never conceded defeat. And that, my friends, is true mettle.

> *The most important element in the character make-up of a man*
> *who is successful is that of mental toughness.*
> COACH VINCE LOMBARDI

I personally saw a team go in the locker room at halftime down by a score of 31 – 3. The team that was ahead had scored every time they got the ball. It looked like they could do anything they wanted. The losing team looked like they had never played football before. Their wheels fell off early and they never got rolling.

At halftime, it was time to test this team's mettle. It was the moment for a "gut check" from every single embarrassed player in that locker room. The coach gave his crew a pretty simple message. He didn't yell. He didn't scream. He said this, "They won the first half, but the game is far from over. Those of you who think this game is over, those of you who don't want to give a 100 percent effort in the second half, you can stay in the locker room."

No one stayed in the locker room. It was time to test their mettle. In all the years I have been watching football, I've never seen such a comeback. The transformation was like Dr. Jekyll and Mr. Hyde. The team that was behind by twenty-seven points tied the game at 34 – 34! As they made up the large deficit, their confidence grew stronger. Because of this one game's outcome—regardless of how far behind they were in future games—these players would always feel they had a chance to win. They could not and would not quit.

Mental toughness is not something people are born with. It is learned through experiences like the one above.

This team did not end up winning this game. They missed a field goal in overtime. But that really didn't matter. Every player and coach involved with this game saw what was possible. They each got a chance to test their mettle, to learn about mental toughness and determination. They discovered it was okay to heat up their mettle a bit and let it bend. They saw that when they kept applying the pressure and giving 100 percent, it didn't break or melt. It just grew stronger. Happens every time!

FOCUSED ANXIETY

The individual performer or team that falls apart when in the heat of competition does so largely because of mental factors like runaway nervousness, intimidation, poor concentration, negativity, anxiety, or an inability to let go of past mistakes or bad breaks. These factors are the real cause of poor performance under pressure. Football players do not struggle because of lack of conditioning, inadequate coaching, or a scarcity of physical skills or ability. Sure, physical or mechanical factors can sometimes cause sub-par play. But the real core of the problem lies in the factors that mentally inhibit one's performance. Even outside of the game of football, these same issues tend to decay, weaken, and break a person's mettle.

If you're a dedicated performer, you've worked too hard and sacrificed too much to let mental weakness disrupt your level of success. The mental toughness you can learn in football and other sports can raise your performance to the level you desire.

For a person to realize their full potential, one has to start training their mind as well as the body. Just as football players develop physical skills and techniques, you can learn to develop the same type of mental skills in your day-to-day life. There is a technique, and it is learnable.

The first skill you need to develop is to stay relaxed under pressure. I call it "focused anxiety." It's having the ability to focus on what's important and block everything else out. This will perfect your ability to handle self-doubts and negative thinking. It will strengthen your resolve to quickly rebound from failures, bad decisions, or mistakes. And, of course, it will strengthen your mettle ten-fold. Here's the three-step technique:

1. Mentally rehearse for any upcoming possibilities so you can stay relaxed under pressure. You do this by first recognizing the negative mental traps that you might be setting for yourself. But don't focus on them. Instead:

2. Focus on developing a positive mental attitude, a go-for-it attitude. Or, as Nike says, "Just do it." Visualize the positive outcomes you want to occur. Then:

3. Create a laser focus that objectively visualizes all possible negative outcomes. Confronting the negative outcomes before they happen will enable you to work your way through them. This way, you'll be prepared to deal with them if they occur.

Truth is, you've already started doing these three steps. Because you're reading this book, you are learning to harness your inner power.

HARNESSING YOUR INNER POWER

We all face situations that test our mental toughness and our readiness. This happens almost every day. Even the smartest, the most creative, and the most skilled can crack under life's many pressures, especially if they concentrate on the wrong things or are unable to quickly let go of mistakes. If you leave the mental side of performance to chance, you're much more vulnerable to performance-inhibiting issues such as excessive nervousness, psych-outs, choking, slumps, blocks, or the devastating weariness that comes from not trying and failing.

PSYCHOLOGICAL PAIN & YOUR METTLE PLATE

Take Steve Jackson for example. He had been involved in football longer than he could recall. As he entered his mid to late teens, his strength, endurance, and skills continued to grow. Steve busted his butt to become really good in football. He became known for his work ethic, consistency, and ability to come through in the clutch. He was the go-to guy, the player the coaches depended on in crunch time. Steve developed a passion to compete and win. He lived to perform and succeed. It was how Steve defined himself. He had big dreams to compete and achieve at the next level.

Then something unthinkable happened…slowly. It wasn't a dramatic moment. It wasn't an obvious, clear-cut injury. He never really felt a pull, a pop, a snap, a break, or anything like that. Perhaps it might have been easier to deal with the situation if he had experienced a defining moment of complete pain. But that never happened. Steve's injury was far more insidious.

One day, after a big game, Steve noticed some pain and tenderness in his leg. "No problem," he thought to himself. In the game of football, you get use to dealing with this kind of stuff. Steve quickly dismissed it as a minor discomfort. The next day in practice, he noticed that his shoulder was tight and sore. "No big deal." He tried to ignore this, too. He attempted to push through the pain. When practice ended, his shoulder was throbbing. He realized that perhaps he was a bit foolish to have forced himself to work through the pain. That night, when Steve couldn't even lift his arm to brush his hair, he started to get worried.

Steve kept telling himself there was nothing really wrong, but the pain just wouldn't quit. As much as he hated to do it, the next day he went to the coach to tell him he was a little hurt. The coach told Steve to take a few days off. Steve was forced to rest. However, even after he took a couple of days off, the first few movements he tried at the next practice just killed him. In fact, the shoulder felt just as tight and sore as before. How bad could it really be? Maybe he just needed to take a little more time off.

The throbbing in Steve's shoulder kept him up several nights in a row. When the pain forced him to miss two more games, he finally got the message. Something was very wrong. It was time to drag his butt to the doctor!

Seeing a sports medicine doctor confirmed Steve's worst fears. His shoulder was really bad. The doctor said that he would have to be out of action for at least two to three months! He explained that Steve had a form of tendonitis and possibly some rotator-cuff problems. He didn't know how long it would take to heal. What he said next really got Steve's attention: "Unless you take care of that shoulder and give it enough rest, you risk doing some permanent damage."

"What does that mean?" Steve asked.

The doctor said, "If you continue to play through the pain, you may be jeopardizing your athletic career."

Steve thought, "Is he crazy? Is he really telling me that I may never play again!!! How could that possibly be?"

Then, instead of focusing on the positive, Steve began to dwell only on the negative. He began to question how he could survive without his daily dose of football. He got anxious. He worried. He became angry and depressed. As a result, Steve never returned to the field. Today he is a gas-station attendant in Lima, Ohio.

If you are an athlete and have had an injury, you know that the physical discomfort is only a small part of the pain you experience in the rehab process. The psychological pain caused by your injury and possible loss of your sport can be far more devastating than the torn ligaments, pulled muscles, ripped cartilage, or broken bones. But you can speed up your overall recovery enormously if you recognize this as psychological pain and focus on positive action instead.

To better understand what happens when an athlete is sidelined because of an injury, it's important to examine the important function that mental toughness plays in your life.

You Are What You Do

Whether you are a serious athlete or a dedicated workaday professional, you might come to see yourself only in terms of your sport or your profession. Whether you were a football player, swimmer, baseball player, skater, tennis player, wrestler, gymnast, lawyer, doctor, teacher, or whatever, it's easy to see your sport or your job as defining who you are.

Without their sport, an athlete can lose their sense of identity and feel they are nothing. Steve did. With his long-term commitment of time, energy, and pain over the years, his sport became the totality of who he was.

If an athlete—or a professional—lets this happens, they missed the secret of football. They'll drive themselves crazily down a dead-end road that leads only to self-pity and destruction. On the other hand, if a person takes all their sports or work experiences with them into life's fifth quarter, they will succeed. Using the valuable lessons they learn, football players' mental toughness will be laid in reinforced cement. Their inner powers will be harnessed. Nothing will be able to meddle with their mettle.

The same goes for anyone, whatever their career may have been. Your inner power is available to you. Your mettle will strengthen to the degree that you understand and apply the secrets of football to your own life.

An Outlet for Anxiety and Stress

There is absolutely no question that participation in sports helps a person handle stress of all kinds. Individuals who have no physical outlets in their life tend to internalize their stress. The individual who has no way to physically "burn" stress out of their body may wind up with stomach problems, headaches, or other physical symptoms. They may even turn to drugs, alcohol, or some other addictive, self-destructive behavior to try to cope.

Furthermore, many athletes discover that their involvement in their sport is a constructive way to escape from the stress of a dysfunctional family or a deprived environment. No place is perfect, there are no perfect parents, and every family has issues. Many households have some level of dysfunction. Statistics show that 60 percent of marriages today end in divorce. None of us get to pick our parents or the situations we grow up in. However, we all have the opportunity to learn from these experiences. We all get the chance to harness our inner power and use its force to propel us forward.

CONSEQUENCES OF THE END

So what happens to a player when their involvement in sports suddenly ends? They might become overwhelmed by a variety of internal and external losses. As the athlete struggles with the impact of these losses, their mettle can start to decompose. The first thing that they might lose is their identity as an athlete and team member. They can become lost in life, with no direction.

Their sport has been their life. Most of their goals were focused in this arena. If they are not constantly in the pool, out on the field, course, or court, practicing and competing in their sport, they question who they are. A college football player sidelined from the sport might think, "I've been playing football since I was eight years old. It's all I know. It's who I am and what I do. If I'm not a football player, then who am I really? What do I do next?"

Without their sport, with its frequent practices and competitions, it is understandable how athletes out of the game suddenly feel a significant vacuum in their lives.

This feeling is far less extreme if they have been able to expand their involvement into other activities of life. Unfortunately, in today's world, most serious athletes have to commit a tremendous amount of time in order to excel in their sport. The level of participation and commitment needed makes other, non-athletic activities a virtual impossibility. And when it's time to put the shoulder pads away, this loss of direction comes with two other significant losses.

METTLE-HEALTH

First, a player can lose their physical health and their sense of invincibility. Many athletes are used to being independent. They rely upon their bodies to respond as trained and directed. At the end of a long career, they have to face the cold, hard fact that their body has somehow failed them.

This can be a tough pill to swallow. Maybe they were a step too slow, didn't grow enough, or had a career-ending injury. If their career ended because their bodies let them down in some way, especially due to injury, this can make them dependent on doctors, trainers, physical therapists, etc. Most athletes have a strong independent streak and hate having to depend on anyone other than themselves.

Secondly, a player can lose a major source of their self-esteem. If they got their thrills from being faster than everyone else, being the best tackler, throwing touchdowns, or shutting an opposing player down, they'll get precious few good feelings from sitting in the stands helplessly watching the action. Instead, their self-doubts can begin to plague them. They may begin to struggle with questions of their own self-worth.

This thought process will deteriorate if they aren't being pushed by coaches in practice. If they aren't working hard on their game and helping their former teams, they might begin to wonder, "What real value do I have?" For many athletes, this is probably the hardest part of ending their careers. It can be a huge blow to their ego. Suddenly, stronger or younger athletes are taking their place and doing what they think they should be doing, but no longer can. This process can occur the same way in any profession in the game of life. But it doesn't have to happen. In fact, just the opposite should occur.

Everyone needs to understand the nature of life. At some point it's time to move on and play a different game. Football players particularly have a leg up on all subsequent successes in the game of life. The mental toughness they learned gives them the ability to make the transition to the working world after they've played their last game. Players usually understand that they need to join a different team—a business team.

There may not be any press or cheering crowds, but they're getting paid well for their efforts. And that can be very gratifying. Anyone leaving his current profession needs to create his next endeavor, whatever it may be. As I have stated before, the big game really never ends. You just join a different team with new rules of engagement! You start in the most important quarter, the one where the game is really won or lost—the fifth quarter.

SEE THE FUTURE

So what does all this mean to anyone whose career ends? If you want to stay on the fast track, you need to harness your inner power and see the future. You need to anticipate that certain feelings and behaviors may emerge as a result of your life changes. You need to understand that these feelings and behaviors are absolutely normal. They are part of the process of developing mental toughness. They are a natural part of successfully coping. As with any kind of loss, players may go through a number of stages related to mourning.

Some sports psychologists feel that these stages parallel Kubler-Ross's five stages of death and dying: denial, anger, bargaining, depression, acceptance. The player may downplay or ignore their true feelings. The player may adopt a "why me" attitude and act hostilely and resentfully to everyone around him. Some athletes then get into an internal bargaining with themselves, i.e. "if I do this and that, then maybe something will change." At some point in this whole process, depression can set in as one comes to fully realize that the game is over for them. The depression may entail a loss of interest in or withdrawal from once-favorite activities, sleep and eating disturbances (sleeping too much/insomnia, overeating/loss of appetite), low energy, and possibly even suicidal thoughts and feelings. At the end of this depression stage, the player comes to accept their situation and make the best of it.

I think instead of going through all these unnecessary stages, the best thing to do is to see the future, plan for the future, and have plan A and plan B all set in your head.

Plan A is simple. You train, do your best, and commit yourself to play at the next level, whatever that level may be.

Plan B is that you have another avenue thought out for yourself. So you couldn't make it as a professional, so what? Life is full of chapters that end. New ones begin! All you have to do is turn the page.

What if you already are a professional, you've reached the top, and your career is ending? There is no plan A option and you don't really relish plan B. Let yourself experience the Ten Professional Strategies for Coping with the End.

Ten Professional Strategies for Coping with the End

1. ALLOW YOURSELF TO BE SAD.

Allow yourself to mourn and feel whatever loss you are experiencing. Being "macho," "strong," or "brave" by burying or hiding your feelings is not only a complete waste of time, it will interfere with you effectively coping and recovering. It's even okay to cry! Dealing with your feelings honestly, in a positive manner is an important part of the process of moving on. Feeling is part of healing!

2. ACCEPT THAT IT IS WHAT IT IS

No amount of wishing upon a star will change the reality of certain situations. Yes, it stinks that time passes and that your career ended too early in life, before you were ready. Yes, it's thrown a huge curve into the path you were following. Unfortunately, this is your reality right now. You have to allow yourself to deal with where you are, right now!

3. SET NEW GOALS FOR YOURSELF

As you begin down your new path, you may very well have to learn to measure your successes very differently than before. It will likely mean that you also have to start at square one to build up a new career, especially if you are going after the same level of success. Develop and focus on new goals. Leave the old ones in the past, where they belong. Revisit the chapter on goal setting.

4. KEEP A POSITIVE MENTAL ATTITUDE (A PMA)

As difficult as this may be, keep a positive mental attitude, a PMA. A person's outlook is everything! A positive attitude can speed up an athlete's transition from professional sports to the game of life. A PMA can also speed up a person's transition from one career to the next. It's all up to you. Avoid being negative, because nothing good ever comes from negativity. Negativity only brings you and everyone else around you down. Revisit the chapter on Attitude.

5. BE PROACTIVE

If you were a professional athlete, you undoubtedly have a network. Now is the time to leverage your contacts. A network is only good if you access it and leverage it. There is no shame in reaching out to people. The best networking plan is to start out with the people who you might be able to help. Always think of others first. In your new role, sometimes you have to give to get. For example, if you're an ex-professional, there are a lot of people who enjoy rubbing elbows with ex-professional athletes. Make this work for you. Stay open to all opportunities. The same goes for anyone outside the world of sports. Look around you and communicate. Former co-workers, neighbors, friends, acquaintances—talk to them. Most people love to help.

6. BE TEAM FRIENDLY

Participate in team functions if and when you can. Fight any urge to isolate yourself. You may suddenly feel different, but chances are you're probably the only one on your former team who thinks this. The worst thing to do when you're in a vulnerable state is to cut yourself off from your group. Make a serious effort to reach out. Don't pull in!

7. BE PATIENT

You didn't become a professional football player overnight. Playing at the professional level means you have achieved the pinnacle of your sport or profession. Be patient and recall the amount of effort and time it took you to reach your level of success. You are way ahead; you are not starting from scratch. Almost everything you have practiced and learned will transition to the real world.

As a player, you had to have mental toughness. Your mettle has been tested for years. It is this time—the fifth quarter of your life—that you have been preparing for.

8. CRY, BABY

When was the last time you had a good cry? Here in the twenty-first century, it's okay for tough guys to cry—so get used to it! Expressing our emotions in a positive or channeled way is one of the healthiest things we can do. Football gives men and boys permission to cry if they are upset. When you've put your heart and soul into something but still come up short, it is upsetting. It is and always will be an emotional experience. It happens to us all, usually multiple times in our lives. To have a commitment that is so deep that it brings tears to your eyes when you fail is not wimpy. In fact, players know it is just the opposite. Disagree with this? Go up to Warren Sapp, the three hundred pound All Pro defensive lineman for the Tampa Bay Buccaneers. Call him a crybaby or a wimp when you see him with tears in his eyes. Then, when you are released from the hospital, call me and let me know how that worked out for you.

9. EXPRESS YOUR EMOTIONS

Football players learn that expressing the gauntlet of emotions is a positive thing, if they are channeled in the right direction. Uncontrolled outbursts of unfocused, unchanneled emotions never have and never will serve any of us. Getting upset and punching the wall is just stupid. First of all, you will likely hurt your hand. Secondly, you will have to spend time and money to repair the wall. Fist fighting with another person only proves you're a moron. You could hurt yourself permanently, hurt the other person permanently, find yourself in a costly lawsuit, or a host of other negative outcomes. What's the best thing that can come out of a street fight? You win the fight and your manhood is kept intact? It's sad if that's how anyone defines their manliness.

In football, there is a lot of potential rage and anger. It tends to be upsetting when someone at a full run knocks you to the ground repeatedly. Also, you can't exactly ask them politely to stop doing that to you. Players learn early from their experiences on the field to channel their feelings. They reach deep down and channel their negative feelings to effect a positive outcome for themselves and their team.

10. APPLY THE SECRETS OF FOOTBALL

A player might feel that they have no skills that are transferable from football to other endeavors. Not true! Recognize all you have learned. It *all* applies to your fifth quarter! This is the essence of what this entire book is about. To excel as a player, you have gradually developed some very powerful attributes of success. These success skills can be readily harnessed to other challenges that you pursue. All football skills that you have learned and mastered are relevant to your next challenge: the fifth quarter.

FOOTBALL—METAPHOR FOR LIFE

Now, let's look in more detail at how football contains parallels to life and success. Let's examine how it teaches each one of the needed lessons early to those who played. You can't turn back the hands of time, but you can rewind your clock.

Ten Similarities Everyone Can Relate to

1. WE ALL LEARN LESSONS: Everyone plays in the game of life. Every day, we are given opportunities to learn lessons. We may not want the lesson or think it is irrelevant; nevertheless, we get them anyway. So it goes in football.

2. THERE ARE NO MISTAKES, JUST LESSONS: Growth is a process of trial and error. We experiment with new things and have mixed results. The experiments that do not net us the results we want or that fail are part of the discovery process of our quest to find out what works. This is an exact correlation to a team's game plan.

3. PRACTICE MAKES PERFECT: New opportunities, lessons, and trials come to us in different forms at different times. They will continue to come our way until we learn them. When we do, we move on to the next one. You'll often see a football team continue to run the same play until the defense figures it out. As soon as the defense figures out how to stop the play, the offense then tries another play. The offense will run that play until the defense learns to stop that one. And so on. The same is true in life.

4. LEARNING NEVER ENDS: Show me a coach who feels they have it all figured out, and I'll show you a losing record. There is no part of life that does not contain ongoing lessons to be learned. If you are breathing, there are always new and exciting lessons to be learned.

5. REFLECTIONS: You can't throw footballs at a glass house when you live in one. In other words, you can't be judgmental of others until you are perfect. We are all perfectly aware that no one is perfect. The things you love or hate about someone else are precisely the things you love or hate about yourself.

6. CHOICES: Even though players are thoroughly coached before their games, what they do on the field is up to them. It's the same in life. Even though everyone has been through tons of life lessons, how you live your life is up to you. We all possess different skills and unique talents. We all have the ability to implement and execute everything contained in this book.

7. YOU HAVE THE ANSWERS: It may take a while for everyone to understand that if you look inside yourself, you will find the answer to every question you now have or ever will have. You are empowered to succeed.

8. GET BACK WHAT YOU GIVE: The effort you put into football or life is in direct proportion to what you get back.

9. HESITATION: He who hesitates is lost—or more succinctly—loses. All it takes is a brief moment of hesitation on the football field and the opportunity is lost. The hole closes for the running back or the defensive player misses a tackle. In life, the same thing happens, only it's usually called risk. Not much has ever been gained by clinging to a false sense of security.

10. HEART: In the game of football, skill and size is only part of the successful mix. The most important muscle in football is heart. Putting your whole heart into whatever you pursue is the best way to guarantee success, both on and off the field.

In my world, it would be crazy to think that every time someone beat me in a sales situation I should go to their company and pound on them. No, I don't think that would accomplish much. Believe me, the same feeling I got when someone cleaned my clock on the football field is the same feeling I get when I lose business, maybe even more so. We can all relate to the physical pain and anger that is sure to follow after someone puts a big hit on you. When someone beats me in business, the anger and emotions can be the same. My solution is to reach inside myself and put the pedal to the metal.

Ask yourself:

- What should I have done differently?

- What can I do better?

- How can I make sure this does not happen again?

- What have I learned from this experience?

We all lose opportunities from time to time. Learn from the experience. Channel your feelings to effect a positive outcome for the next time. Just like a football player, you need to pick yourself up, dust yourself off and go right back at it.

Each of us has a degree of mental toughness. Some more than others, but we all have it. Access your mental toughness whenever you need to, but more important, continue to work at making it stronger and stronger every day.

CHAPTER TWELVE

HALL-OF-FAMERS

LEADERSHIP

The leader can never close the gap between himself and the group.
If he does, he is no longer what he must be.

COACH VINCE LOMBARDI

Threre are hundreds of books, seminars, groups, and classes, all focused on defining leadership. My definition of a leader is someone who has mastered and follows the principle attributes of success that are the foundation to the secrets of football. A leader not only understands these attributes, they apply them in all aspects of life because these attributes are part of his or her core being. This inspires others to trust and believe and emulate his or her actions. The great leaders I have studied have two things that separate them from others. One, they are very compassionate people. Two, they all have great integrity.

Compassion means understanding and having empathy for others. It's the ability to put yourself in the other person's shoes or (cleats). It doesn't mean you have to agree with everything the other person says or does, or that you have to buy into whatever they might be selling you. It does include being able to assess any situation objectively and analytically.

Integrity can be measured and defined in many ways. A leader must respect legitimate authority and know how to stay between the lines that have been laid down. A leader knows how to move these lines by working closely and cooperating with whoever set them. To be a leader you need to abide by the rules and support the good, ignoring personal bias or individual needs.

FOOTBALL LEADERS

Football gives players the opportunity to learn the basics of leadership. Some people are natural leaders; to others, it is a learned trait or skill. In this world you are either a leader or a follower. It is just that black and white.

In football most of the leaders of the team are usually upperclassmen. It's not normal for a freshman to walk in and become an immediate leader.

So most often the leaders are the older team members, the guys with more maturity who set a positive example. They can't go out there and break all the rules of the university and all the rules of the football team and expect to be a team's true leader.

STATISTICAL LEADERS VERSUS REAL LEADERSHIP

Every team has statistical leaders. These are the players who have the big numbers: most yards, most tackles, most interceptions, most completions, etc. They usually get a lot of recognition and glory for being the statistical leader. Statistical leaders are typically the better players with the most skills and talents. But does this mean they are leaders on and off the field as we have defined leadership? The answer is no. You would think if you were one of the best players on the team you would inspire, help, encourage, and be the role model for the rest of the team. Sometimes this is the case because the statistical leaders typically work harder and are the most dedicated players. But not always.

There was a situation recently in the NFL involving a receiver who will remain nameless. He was a first-round draft choice a few years back. Because he constantly complained about not getting the ball thrown to him enough, he was eventually traded, even though he was a statistical leader and one of the best receivers in the league. (He led his team in most, if not all, receiving categories.) Despite his multi-million dollar contract and more than half the season left to play (and pay), his coach suspended him from the team and sent him home.

Even if you're a great guy, statistical leadership is often short lived. Records are made and broken everyday. You might have the hot hand or the eye for the ball, but it won't last forever. When you are on that roll, it's wise to assert yourself as a team or group leader. Give the credit to the ones around you who helped you gain your statistics. That's what winning leaders do versus losers who only think about their stats and breaks their arms patting themselves on the back.

Sometimes, statistical leaders who are losers don't care about the team or the others around them. They are focused on themselves first and everything else is a far second. Some statistical leaders become or are, very self-centered and embody exactly the opposite traits needed to be a team or group leader.

BUSINESS LEADERSHIP

Statistical leaders transcend the world of sports. There are statistical leaders everywhere you go. Every company has their top sales person, top manager, top services persons, top you-name-it. Their leadership is based on the numbers, their specific statistical measurements.

If you ask a CEO of most major corporations today what their company lacks most of all, what do you think the answer would be? More prospects, more products, more technology, more communication, and more quality? All these would likely make the list. However, what you would hear most often is that organizations lack leadership. With good leadership all those other things will come together and fall into place. Leadership determines a company's vision, quality, integrity, work ethic, its environment, attitude, focus, and everything in between. Show me a company with exceptional leadership in all departments, in all roles, and I will show you an organization worth investing in.

Organizations worldwide are confronting more turbulent markets, more demanding shareholders, and more discerning customers. And many are restructuring to meet such challenges. Their success in making these required changes depends heavily on the quality of their leadership, not only at the top of the organization, but also among all managers responsible for operating results.

BEYOND THE MOTIVATION

At all levels of management, leaders possess the ability to motivate people around them. They can motivate them to work a little harder, to put out a little more effort, and they can convince them they are worthy of the task at hand. This doesn't mean every morning before they start work they have to rally all the troops or stand on the desk with a new fire-and-brimstone speech. Nor does it mean the coach or the team leader has to do a song and dance before every game or at half time.

Of course there is absolutely nothing wrong with inspirational talks to generate excitement and enthusiasm. They can have a terrific short-term effect on people. However, short-term motivation can be superficial and dependent on incentives. Sometimes this kind of motivation gives up in the face of serious obstacles. The player might be ready to go out and conquer the world after a riveting motivational speech from their coach. If on the first play of the game, the opposition has a great play or a big hit, all of a sudden those motivational words are quickly forgotten. Mike Tyson was quoted as saying, "Everyone has a plan and is motivated until they get hit in the mouth!"

In the corporate world when we are talking to prospects about our training courses we always differentiate our workshops by explaining that we incorporate motivation within four categories to make it stick. The categories are:

- Theory
- Process
- Motivational
- Ours

Theory refers to the type of training most like a college course. Think inverted triangles, and inner locking circles chock full of conceptual data. It would be like someone handing your football team a book on the theory of the forward pass and saying "now go out and win the game." It is very interesting information, but that alone will not be enough. It certainly is not enough to effect change.

Process is when everything lines up perfectly. It's like a mathematical equation. If A+B=C then C+D=E. This type of training doesn't provide any direction about how to get A and B to begin with. It also makes the assumption that everything is going to turn out according to the pretty formula on the page. However, in the real world, things don't always work out exactly the way you want or think they will. If they did, then a football team would only need a couple of plays because the X's and O's would line up just like they are drawn on the board and every play would work to perfection. Obviously, that's not how it works.

Motivational training is a feel-good session. There is usually some loud up-beat music involved, a speaker, and sometimes some group hugging. It's a lot of fun, and most often, some good things come out of these types of sessions.

However, if all a football team needed was a good motivational speech there would be no reason to play the game. The game would be decided in the locker room. The coach or player who gives the best speech wins! Motivation by itself is like a shower. It might be needed at the time and feel good while you are taking it, but you will need another one tomorrow, and the next day, and the day after too. The same is true for the game on any corporate field.

Results-orientated training is what most organizations need and want. Those other types of training approaches have their place and offer some benefit. Results are what every company, every team, and every person needs. This is the type of training that offers the concept, the theory behind it, and real-life examples demonstrating how it works. It doesn't stop there because then you have to practice what you have learned and—most importantly—it explains in detail how to apply it out in the world. Then you have a plan that impacts the results everyone is seeking.

Football teams operate this way. They draw it up, top it off with an explanation of the concept, stir it up by going out and practicing, sprinkle a little motivation on top, and then they go out and win the game.

PURPOSEFUL ACTION

Purposeful action is the conscious effort put forward in the pursuit of fulfilling an objective. An example of purposeful action on the football field would be an offensive lineman blocking a defensive lineman with the objective of creating an opening for the running back to dart through on his way to the end zone.

For purposeful action in the workplace, managers must engage a more powerful attribute, their determination. Professors from the London Business School found that most managers they interviewed were motivated to achieve their goals. Yet only 10 percent of them demonstrated volition, the ability to take purposeful action to implement their goals. Effective leaders who demonstrate these actions:

- Give people a vivid picture of the task at hand in order to activate their emotions.

- Help people confront their ambivalence. Instead of painting an unrealistic view by offering only motivation, they actively prepare people to address the obstacles they will face or are facing.

- Prevent people from becoming limited to only one way of achieving desired results by helping them to see and exploit a wider range of choices.

- Build in rules for "cutting bait" to counteract the blinders that appear when an overzealous personal commitment to a course of action might obstruct more viable options.

- Encourage people to change something that isn't working. It is not prudent to keep investing one's time and talents in unprofitable actions without making measurable changes.

EMULATE A WINNER

A football player never starts out as an upper classman or as the team's leader. At some point they are a follower. Football teaches players how to become effective leaders and gives them the chance to lead their team. It's a hard-hitting opportunity that molds every football player every day—in practice and playing on the field.

It's the same out in the world. Leaders aren't typically born, they are molded. You don't have to be on a football team to shape-up and become a leader. Here's what you can do.

- Read about other leaders. Find out what they do to inspire people to follow them. Then do some of those things yourself.

- Carefully choose a leader you personally know that you can emulate. Be sure to choose a winner. "Winner" can be defined in different ways. You can be a winner in a game or a statistical leader, but not be a worthy role model. So, before deciding who to emulate, choose your arena carefully. Remember:

1. Who you choose to associate with will make a difference in the path you choose for yourself.

2. Your friends and associates are a direct reflection of who you are.

3. People you hang around with will either pull you up or drag you down.

WATCH OUT FOR THE PEOPLE-FEEDERS, TOXIC SUCKERS, AND TWO-FACED MONSTERS

Sounds like a horror film, doesn't it? Your life will become one if you decide to follow the wrong leader. So learn to recognize these types—fast! People feeders are those you'll find in relationships that feed off each other negatively. No two individuals are alike, and often people get together because one's strength is the other's weakness and visa versa. These people feast on each other's self-esteem and often devour and destroy each other in the process. On the flip side, people who augment each other's lives and help others flourish and prosper are true potential leaders. They are called "mentors," and they often more available and eager to help than you might realize. Seek them out

A positive mentoring relationship occurs when one person asks another for help, gets this help, and accepts it. You see this type of leadership relationship every weekend during football season. How many times have you watched a game and the veteran starting quarterback is out of the game but does everything he can to help the back-up QB learn the hot reads and the different coverages? This type of mentoring relationship is healthy and should be encouraged.

The ones you have to watch out for are the toxic types. These are the people who are just hanging around, sucking the life out of you, secretly poisoning your confidence with their covert remarks because they would really like to see you fail. These are the jealous "wanna be's," who always have a sarcastic comment or offer nothing back of value. Evaluate all your relationships and limit your exposure to anyone you think might be toxic. Trust your gut feeling. If you think someone is even a little bit toxic, they probably are.

The two-faced monsters are harder to spot. These are the people who are saying good things to you when they are around, but tend to talk negatively about everyone else. Don't be naïve and think they won't or don't talk about you when you are not present. This trait is a sign of insecurity, one trait a good leader does not have.

To help you evaluate these three types of people, all you have to really do is look and listen.

LOOK

When it comes to choosing a good leader, look closely! That person might look good from a distance, but with closer observation, he or she turns out to be far from optimum. Take your time and be patient. It is far better to be selective and get it right verses wasting time laying a foundation that you can't build on.

Look for people with compassion and integrity. They drop little clues all the time by how they treat other people. These small actions will add up and it will be easy for you to see the score. How do they treat the maid, the bellman, waiters, parking attendants and bar tenders? Are they in the habit of saying thank-you, please, or do they just bark out orders, acting as if the people supplying the service are lucky to have the privilege of waiting on them?

LISTEN

Evaluate if they are consistently talking and rarely listening. Determine if they are honest and genuine or if they are professional bull-slingers. People who try to outwardly impress you are those you might want to steer clear of. On the other hand, don't let your "Happy Ears" (which is just hearing what you want to hear) dub in a glossy interpretation of what people tell you. Sometimes, it's hard not to do this, especially when you hope a person is as wonderful as they appear to be or are as they tell you they are.

You will find the most talented, wealthiest people are almost embarrassed to flaunt their success. Genuinely successful people sometimes go out of their way to hide their good fortune. The ones that tell you how great they are and wear their resume of accomplishments on their foreheads are the ones you for sure do not want to emulate. Always look and listen and remember that sometimes less noise means more true leadership.

When it came time to choose his college, Robbie had to listen to the "noise." He had a choice between a few different schools that wanted him to play football for them. He had narrowed it down to two schools. One was closer to home. It had a very high, noisy fun-factor (in other words, it is a party school) and their football program got more national recognition. However, their academic standards were low. The requirements, if I remember correctly, were that you had to be able to at least sign your name with an X and be able to play football.

The other school was Rice University which has unparalleled academic standards. They turn kids away every year who are not able to meet their high educational standards. Rice plays a big-time schedule, facing teams like Oklahoma, Michigan, Texas, Nebraska, Michigan State, Boise State, Hawaii, TCU, and several others. Even with all this, it still was not as notable as the alternative school he was considering. So if you are eighteen years old, which opportunity looks most appealing to you? Let's party, right?

Robbie was graced with some good advice from a player named Benji Woods. Benji had gone to Robbie's high school, had played football, had attended the "party school," and then transferred to Rice. He offered some sage advice. He told Rob, "If you hang out around trash, pretty soon you will start to smell like it regardless of your qualities." He was right and my son was smart enough to look and listen, and so he went to Rice.

YOUR LOOK-AND-LISTEN LEADERSHIP QUESTIONNAIRE

Here is a simple checklist you can use to choose a potential leader or someone you might associate yourself with.

1. Do I trust them by their actions?

2. Would I like to be perceived by my actions in the same way they are perceived?

3. Do they have traits and skills I can learn from?

4. Do I like their manners and the way they treat other people ?

5. Do people respect this person for all the right reasons?

If you answered no to any of these questions, this is probably not your best option for a leadership role model. You can apply the same questionnaire to the people you currently have in your circle of influence. The same is true for them as well. If you answered no to just one of these questions, you might want to evaluate the nature of your relationship. There are millions of worthwhile people in the world that you can benefit from. Be critical in your selection process. Choosing the right people to associate with is critical to your future health, spiritual well-being, and prosperity.

LEAD BY EXAMPLE

How can you begin, right *now*, to help those you love and care about become a leader? The answer is in three words: lead by example. Are you a parent? A teacher? A coach? An associate? A friend? Molding leadership starts at home with parents, then travels to schools where teachers can help, then on to the sports arena where coaches can contribute, and then out to the world where we choose friends and associates.

As a parent, the saying, "Do as I say, not as I do" never resonated or rang true for me. I did my best to plant the seeds of leadership and consistently add water to insure their flowers bloom. Unfortunately, not all parents have good leadership skills or played football. They can't plant seeds they don't have. If that is the case, parents can still help carve out the mold for leadership. Simply set a good example.

This pertains to players, parents, coaches, teachers, you, and me. It is unreasonable to expect anyone to follow you when you are on a different or rocky path. If you smoke and drink, but preach to the others around you they shouldn't, that is a contradiction. If you are in a leadership role at work, it is unreasonable to think that if you start work at 10:00 a.m. and leave at 4:00 p.m., others are going to put longer hours in or work harder. This is just basic common sense, but for some reason this concept of leading by example is lost on a lot of people who are in leadership roles.

A person isn't a good leader just because they are in a leadership role. True leaders on the field represent themselves, their team and their coaches by leading by example. They are in the weight room working out and watching films during their free time. They are in bed early, resting up for the next day's practice or game. A true leader lives in a glass house, regardless of the world they live in. Lead by example!

LEADERSHIP FROM THE BAD EXAMPLES

Maybe you're a person who does not have a positive role model. Let's say you have not done the research as suggested, reading the biographies and history of other leaders because they are too remote and hard for you to relate to. You can still grow into an effective and powerful leader. As was mentioned before, we can learn something from every person we come in contact with.

Some lessons can be learned by observing and watching people's bad habits or weak examples of leadership. You might not know exactly what to do or how to lead, but you can easily watch others to see what not to do. Robbie had football players on his high school team who got stoned or did other drugs before games. They were the upper classmen and the statistical leaders. They looked like they were having fun and always did pretty well in the games. Regardless, it didn't take a brain surgeon to figure out this was an example of bad leadership. Unfortunately, today there are more bad examples of poor leadership than positive role models. A leader in training who has great potential will be able to recognize these bad examples and leverage them, adding them to their mental file of things not to do. However, it is often hard for a young, impressionable person to discern the differences between glitz, glamour, and genuine good.

I personally find it easier to see mistakes, bad habits, and mismanagement versus good examples of leadership. Bad examples tend to stand out a little more and they are much more prevalent in today's society. But, it's my business to help companies weed out the problem, so I'm highly attuned to these good or bad habits. Strive to take something away from every person you meet and every relationship you have.

STAND ALONE

A lot of times a leader must stand on their own. A leader cannot concern themselves with winning a popularity contest. It is optimal if everyone loves a leader and respects them. More times than not, these two objectives oppose each other. A leader has to be respected first and foremost. Leadership cannot always be a democracy. If it were, then each time a decision was made, there would have to be a consensus to move forward. In football, this would mean that every time a coach calls a time out (I guess he would have to even get a consensus to do that under our democracy leadership plan), he would have to call the entire team over and get everyone's opinion and agreement on what the next play should be. Then he would have to make sure everyone felt good about the call. We'll have to extend timeouts to be about thirty-minutes long from now on if we are going to lead in this way.

A leader has to be able to make quick, decisive decisions based on the information they have at the time, which includes data they incorporate from their past experiences. It is unrealistic to think everyone is going to agree with or like the decision. A great example of this type of stand-alone leadership was portrayed in the movie *Remember the Clash of the Titans*.

The movie is the true story of the 1971 forced integration of all-white T.C. Williams High School in Alexandria, Virginia. Racial strife envelopes the community and tempers flair when a black football coach, Herman Boone, is brought in to replace the white coach, Bill Yoast. Yoast stays on as assistant coach hoping to see Boone fail at his attempts to win over the team and the community. This is a perfect example of a toxic relationship. Boone has no idea that the school board has struck a deal that they can fire him after his first loss. This issue never becomes a problem because the team keeps winning and makes it to the state finals.

The two coaches don't see eye-to-eye on the best way to manage the team. Boone is a charismatic leader with a brutal, military-style approach to coaching. He believes in breaking the players down and then re-building them as a team. Yoast is more laid-back and conservative, and feels Boone is pushing the players too hard. This difference in coaching styles leads to several confrontations between the two coaches and between the players.

Boone is an excellent example of a leader. He knows he faces a tough challenge and has to be a stand-alone leader in order to instill a will-to-win in his controversial team. Instead of giving in to the nay-sayers, Boone pushes his team to be their best and focuses on relationships rather than race. His vision for the team involves getting the players interested in what the team is going to become, not what it has been. Just like all good leaders he has the ability to see all sides of an issue and to eliminate biases. Yoast, on the other hand, plays the role of the manager. He is not interested in change but wants to keep things the way they've always been. His leadership philosophy is basically, "if it isn't broken, why fix it?"

Boone also uses both power and authority as a leader. Power is the strength or force to exercise control to get people to do something, while authority is power that is accepted as legitimate by subordinates. The white players do not immediately accept Boone's authority. Many threaten to quit the team if Boone remains as head coach, and their parents threaten to move their children to other schools. Boone must use power to force the players to tolerate each other until he can help them look beyond the conflict. At training camp and as the season progresses, the players increasingly respect his leadership, and they no longer see his power as illegitimate.

While many people seek to avoid conflict, leaders realize conflict can bring an opportunity for change or revitalization. Coach Boone knew when to amplify conflict, when to escalate conflict, and when to move the team away from divisiveness and toward a vision of the common good.

If you didn't already understand the saying, "It is lonely at the top," this story might help to illuminate its meaning. It is not always easy to be an effective leader. It is especially hard when the leaders plan and vision are not realized. A good leader will also take the blame for not achieving the results and give the glory to others when they do. Leadership can be a lonely place, but to many, there is not an alternative if they have to choose between leading or following. Leaders control their own destiny. Choose your leadership mentors wisely and walk your path with confidence. Be a leader!

THE ACID TEST FOR LEADERSHIP

Below I'm giving you list of the attributes and actions of a leader. Read them and grade yourself. If you can say "yes I do that" to a majority of the list, you are a leader. If you want to improve your leadership skills, hold yourself accountable to this list. Most importat, review it periodically to measure how you are progressing. The choice is yours, to lead or follow.

Your Leadership Check List

- Honest
- Build
- Give
- Give approval
- Listen
- Be respectful to those
- Be forgiving
- Care about your teammates
- Problem solve
- Be constructive, not destructive
- Be sincere
- Be thankful
- Have and display courage
- Be courteous
- Help without being asked
- Be kind
- Give well thought-outSet goals
- Be sensitive to others
- Communicate
- Have a good attitude
- Let others speak and share
- Have purpose
- Create a future
- Seek the wisdom of elders
- Be a friend

- Politeness
- Share
- Ask questions
- Stay on task
- Create a vision
- Be open to learning
- Care about your team
- Offer your assistance
- Work together
- Be yourself
- Think before you speak
- Graciousness
- Have integrity
- Cherish the moment
- Take a stand
- Get engaged
- Be attentive
- Ponder alternatives
- Set time limits
- Be positive
- Think creatively
- Be smart
- Welcome change
- Apologize
- Be a mentor

- Ask why
- Accomplish something
- Promote others
- Be loyal
- Set high standards
- Appreciate and create camaraderie
- Have pride
- Challenge yourself
- Be successful
- Give others a chance to lead
- Lead by example
- Seek guidance
- Be successful

- Make commitments
- Practice generosity
- Be patient
- Challenge others
- Have enthusiasm
- Be flexible
- Be loyal
- Challenge others
- Set high standards
- Take calculated risks
- Listen to feelings
- Give feedback
- Challenge yourself

The game of football instills and demands every one of these items from both coaches and players. Leadership can be learned early and applied early through the game of football. There are a lot of leaders who transition these skills, born on the football field, to become true leaders in their life's fifth quarter.

The acid test for leadership is to be consistent. A leader has to posses everything we discussed up to this point and consistency is the key. You cannot be a leader one day, give up, and then try to lead the day after. Most people won't follow that type of example. Have faith and confidence, and be true to yourself and to others around you. By doing this you will have a flock of followers pushing you up the mountain. The view from the top can be spectacular—especially when you share all you see with those who emulate, trust, and follow you.

Choose your leaders well!

Better yet, become one.

CHAPTER THIRTEEN

THE 5TH QUARTER

SUCCESS AND THE SECRETS
OF FOOTBALL

If you settle for nothing less than your best, you will be amazed
at what you can accomplish in your life.

COACH VINCE LOMBARDI

By now you know I fervently believe that football is the greatest game on earth because it is truly a metaphor for life. Whether you have ever participated in sports—playing on the field or supporting your favorite player from the sidelines—hopefully you now understand the secret of football, and you agree it is found in the twelve principal attributes of success we've covered in this book. If you've never played football before and this is the first time you're reading about it, I hope you've come to appreciate the game, and that you also truly understand its secret.

Your application of the principals you've read about will determine how successful you will be throughout all facets of your life. I certainly hope you will all do the exercises in this book and apply each "secret" to your all-important fifth quarter.

If you were a football player at any level, you have already had the opportunity to lay a great foundation for your success in the fifth quarter. All you have to do is to continue applying the principles you learned in football. You need to take the lessons and disciplines that are a part of football and apply them every day to the real game, the game of life.

In case you're wondering about Robbie Beck's fifth quarter, let me tell you what happened—he excelled in every possible way and achieved every goal he set for himself as a college football player. Just a few of his many accomplishments include: starting the very first game of the season as a true freshman, being awarded Newcomer of the Year award, being voted offensive player of the year his junior year, and being elected captain of the team his senior year. Robbie rewrote Rice's record book in several categories including the number two all-time-leader in touchdowns, number two in scoring, the number four all-time leading rusher (pretty amazing as a fullback), holding a five-yard-per-carry average throughout his entire college career and too many others to list. Throughout his football career, Robbie also maintained a double major in Business and Kinesiology and graduated with a 3.0 average.

Robbie's final day on Rice's field was an emotional one. He'd started playing football when he was six years old and now here he was playing his last college game. That was a hard fact to face. Nothing made me happier or brought me more joy than watching him run down the field. The thought that this might be the last time I'd ever see him play brought tears to my eyes.

The day was perfect, a sunny sixty-five degrees in November. To make the event even better, Robbie was one of the field captains for this final football game. All the senior parents were at the game hugging and reflecting on the last four years. It truly was a special day.

There I was with my family and my crying towel close by. To my surprise there was no sadness! First of all Robbie had eighty yards on six carries and two touchdowns in the first quarter. He finished the day with 108 yards on twelve carries and three touchdowns. The Rice team was amazing, falling just short of an all-time NCAA rushing record with their 671 yards of total offense. They also had thirty first downs in their forty-nine to fourteen rout. All the seniors were having the time of their lives. They switched positions, called some plays and everyone got into the action. Robbie was laughing and hugging his teammates and was all smiles. When I stopped to think what he had accomplished throughout his college career and then watching him on the sidelines of this final game, it was hard to be sad about anything. I was actually feeling just the opposite emotion. I was happy! I was happy for Robbie, the team, the coaches, and all the players.

I knew at that moment that Robbie had learned all the principles of success that are in this book. More importantly, he had exercised each one and lived them fully. All he would have to do was transition what he learned and experienced in football to the fifth quarter of his life and the world would be his oyster. How could I be sad in any way?

Shortly after he graduated Rice, the Raiders offered Robbie an opportunity to play eight games in the European NFL, and then join their training camp. A dream come true? It might have been my dream, but it wasn't Robbie's.

Rob had achieved his goal to play college football, and now he wanted to start his fifth quarter beyond the game. So I wasn't surprised when he told me he was turning down the NFL offer. He said, "Dad I'm graduating Rice University with two degrees. I have learned what I needed from football and now it's time for me to move on."

Robbie Beck understood the secret of football! He was committed to new goals he had set for himself, and he was disciplined enough to adhere to them. Even though I would have accepted that NFL contract, Robbie was choosing to succeed on his own terms.

Having taken every opportunity to learn from every experience up to this point in his life, Robbie was in the driver's seat, steering his own bus, with the right attitude, a well-honed competitive spirit, a laser-focus, creativity, courage, and pure mettle. He knew the secret of football.

Earlier in the week before his last game Robbie was quoted in the paper as saying, "Football has taught me a lot about responsibility and how to be a leader. Now that my football career is coming to a close, it puts life into perspective for me. I will take with me the lessons I've learned from football and apply them to other aspects of my life." Gee, if I would have known that he already understood the secrets of football I could have skipped writing this book. Not really. I am proud that he does understand what the game is all about, but there are so many others who never quite connect the dots, so I've written this book for them, too.

Robbie is now twenty-seven years young and works for a very successful telecommunications company, called Cbeyond. He has been promoted several times, earns a six-figure income, and has some fifty people working for him. Robbie has already purchased his first house and was married in September to the love of his life, Celerina. He is active in his community and he cares about the world and its future. Robbie Beck is applying all he has learned from the secrets of football and is indeed succeeding in the fifth quarter!

So can you.

Everyone starts the fifth quarter to his or her life at some point. Everyone gets to make the decision to play or watch life go by. The ones who watch, who wonder "what if…" they just take what comes their way and hope for the best. They typically don't make waves and they have a large equipment bag full of reasons why they need to stay out of the game. There's nothing really wrong with watching a game, but if it's your life you're observing, it will be impossible for you to realize your full potential. In the game of life, even the best observer will not equal the feats of the weakest player.

Every player can participate in the game to the best of their ability. They can apply the principle attributes of success that have been detailed throughout this book. A player will seldom execute every aspect to perfection and will need to continue to try to hone their skills. Just like a football player, everyone needs to practice and improve every week. A player in the game of life will have setbacks and will get knocked down from time to time. That is just part of the game. It is rare that anyone wins every situation they are in—just as no football player has every won ever game. However, as long as they keep working hard, keep a positive mental attitude, and keep applying the attributes of success, they will dance in the end zone of success more times than not!

On the football field, the goal line beckons every player. Everything they do in practice is aimed at crossing that line. How often they cross it will determine if they win or lose the game. In the fifth quarter, that goal line is also there for all of us to cross. Everything you do in preparation during your day to day life sets your path and your ability to cross the goal line you've set for yourself. How far reaching you set that goal, and how you work to get there using the secret of football, will determine how far you go in your fifth quarter.

It's the fifth quarter of one's life that demonstrates the true measure of anyone's game. It's the fifth quarter that is the true challenge of one's life. It's the fifth quarter that really counts. As long as you stay true to the lessons and principles you have learned in this book—in other words, by understanding the secret of football—the fifth quarter will also be the most rewarding one in your life.

For those of you who have determined that you want to be a player in the fifth quarter good for you! Start practicing your end zone dance because you will get a chance to perform it sooner than you might think. To help you get over the goal line sooner rather than later there are some daily exercises I am going to strongly suggest you perform.

DAILY EXERCISE

Unlike many exercise programs that require at least a forty-five minute-per-day commitment, this one will only take you about thirty seconds a day. Surely you have thirty seconds a day to impact the rest of your life.

STEP 1. REVIEW YOUR PROGRAM TO SUCCESS

Review the principle attributes of success. I've listed them below and then given you a score sheet below that. As you review the attributes of success, grade yourself on each attribute. A score of one is poor and a score of ten is the best.

The Secret of Football

PRINCIPLE ATTRIBUTES OF SUCCESS

1. Choosing to succeed
2. Commitment

3. Discipline and Setting Goals

4. Increasing Knowledge

5. Attitude

6. Confidence

7. Competitive spirit

8. Focus

9. Creativity

10. Courage and Character

11. Mental Toughness

12. Leadership

Principle Attributes to Success

SCORE SHEET

Choosing to Succeed_____

Commitment_____

Discipline and Setting Goals_____

Increasing knowledge_____

Attitude_____

Confidence_____

Competitive Spirit_____

Focus_____

Creativity_____

Courage and Character _____

Mental Toughness_____

Leadership_____

STEP 2. MAKE COPIES OF THE "ATTRIBUTES TO SUCCESS SCORE SHEET"

Make copies of the "Attributes To Success Score Sheet" and put them in your office, by your bed, or where ever you will be sure to grade yourself every single day.

STEP 3. GRADE YOURSELF

Grade yourself on how you feel you did compared to the day before, then grade yourself at least every week. Be honest with your grade. The only person who is going to look at this is you. Don't cheat yourself! Be critical and be hard on yourself. This is the only way you are going improve and effect change. It takes three weeks to form a habit so start grading yourself everyday as part of your routine. Pretty soon this will become second nature for you

STEP 4. MAKE A SUCCESS-PLANNING NOTEBOOK

Use this notebook for your Attributes of Success Score sheets. Get notebook dividers and divide this notebook into twelve months. At the end of each month go back and review your progress. Also keep your written goals in this notebook so that everything you need is all in one place.

STEP 5. DEVELOP AN IMPROVEMENT PLAN

Get better! Develop an improvement plan for any area with a consistently low grade. The first thing is to go back and reread the chapter you are having issues with. If that isn't enough to help you make the needed changes, go to the library or bookstore and find another book that focuses just on the particular area you are having issues with.

STEP 6. FIND A COACH

If you are not making the improvements you need from doing step five, just like in the game of football, find a coach. Assess your contacts and figure out who you might know who is strong in the area you are struggling with. Every one of us has different strengths and weaknesses.

STEP 7. ASK FOR HELP

Most people would be flattered if you asked them to help you. It is human nature to help people, but not so easy to ask for help. Asking for help is far from a sign of weakness. It is actually a sign of strength. It takes courage and strength to admit you might need help with something. A lot of people perceive asking someone to help them as a risk. They risk rejection or they are afraid to appear weak or foolish. The only foolish thing is not asking! If you doubt that it is human nature to want to help even a little bit, go out in the middle of street and raise the hood of your car. I will wager ten times the price of whatever you paid for this book someone will come along and help you.

STEP 8. DON'T GET DISCOURAGED

Don't give up and don't get discouraged! Change is not easy. Don't expect miracles to happen over night. Life is a marathon race not a sprint. You do need to get started right away though.

STEP 9. GET STARTED NOW

Procrastination will hurt you. Start your twelve-step plan for success as soon as you finish this chapter. The more you put it off the more likely two negative outcomes will result: one is you won't follow the plan at all. The second is you won't get to perform your victory dance in the end zone of life as soon or as often as you would like.

STEP 10. SHARE YOUR SUCCESS WITH FRIENDS

Shout out your glory! Don't brag about the changes you have made and the outcomes you are enjoying, but it is my advice to let people know you are doing well. Remember the rule, you get what you give. So if you can help someone else by sharing what you have learned from reading this book and applying the principle attributes of success every day, pass it on! You might be surprised what you get back.

STEP 11. CELEBRATE

That's right. Celebrate! Go ahead and reward yourself as you improve and strengthen your weak areas. There is nothing wrong with giving yourself positive motivation. Take a short break, a relaxing vacation. Then, go back at it. I am absolutely sure if you follow this twelve-step program religiously you will see a positive change in your life. What do you have to lose? We already agreed you could take thirty seconds out of your day to impact the rest of your life. Go get your notebook now.

STEP 12. SHARE YOUR THOUGHTS AND SUCCESS WITH ME.

After every training class my company gives I receive e-mails from attendees who let me know how the sales approach we gave them is working for them. It absolutely makes my day every time I receive one of those e-mails. So please e-mail me and share how this program and book is helping you at bbeck@salesbuilders.com. Thanks in advance!

CHAPTER FOURTEEN

POST-GAME

NOTES FROM THE SIDELINES

I started to secretly write this book after Robbie's junior year in high school. At that point I had never written a book, but knew I wanted to offer him at least the gift of understanding and to reveal the secret of football.

255

Robbie didn't have a great junior football season in high school so I was very concerned about him achieving his goal of playing Division I college football. As you know by now I feel strongly and believe passionately that football is a microcosm of real life. It is an excellent way for players to get a feel for how the real world operates and to establish a foundation for greatness when the game ends for them regardless of their age. Parents can and should leverage the football experience and lessons learned to help their kids establish this foundation.

Robbie had worked his tail off between his junior and senior year. As parents we usually have to push our kids a little to get them off the video games or the Internet to go out and do something productive. This wasn't the case with Robbie. He had his sights set on something and he was going to achieve it. He worked-out for three to four hours a day, ate right, took the right supplements, and would get up the next morning and hit it again. I have always told the kids if they want something bad enough, regardless of what it is, if they are willing to sacrifice to the level required, in the end, they will realize their dreams. I believe this whole heartedly and live my life by it.

The percentage of kids who receive Division I full scholarships is very low. The percentage drops even further if you are under sized for their position. Finally, the percentage drops to almost zero if the kid goes out and gets hurt his senior year in high school. So all of these thoughts started to creep into my mind: what do I say to Robbie if he busts his butt and he doesn't achieve his goal? I could just hear myself saying, "Well, son, sometimes you put your heart into something and give it everything you got and it just doesn't work out." Even though that can be the case from time to time, as we all know, that was not the life lesson I want to give my eighteen-year-old son or any of my kids.

I started to consider my daughter, Melissa, and how strong her desire was to realize her dreams. My sons Tyler and Nick are also going to have to go out and survive in the big world soon, too. So I started this book to make sure they all understood how they could learn the attributes of success in their own fifth quarters.

As I started to write it I realized there were more players out in the world who didn't really understand the secret of football, and so I continued to expand my thoughts and message to reach parents and their kids and professionals in every field.

Lucky for me, Robbie afforded me four extra years to write this book. As you have read, he did achieve the goal he set for himself—receiving a full Division I college football scholarship to Rice University, going on to excel as an athlete and a student and then—knowing his true path and following it forward into his fifth quarter.

A Letter to Robbie

I miss Friday nights and Saturday afternoons watching my son play football. When Robbie was in high school, I used to get to the stadium two hours before the game started. Regardless of how important a business meeting I might be in on Friday was, or what my workload was, starting about noon I mentally geared up for the game. One Friday I was extremely busy and couldn't focus on the upcoming game. I still arrived at the stadium about an hour early, but was very concerned what kind of game Robbie would have since I hadn't mentally prepared. He had his usual stellar performance and the team won. It was then that I realized that I wasn't playing, so my mental preparation really wasn't needed—that took me a long time to figure out.

However, all through high school, I used to have this ritual with Robbie. I would either buy him an inspirational card or on occasion make him one. I made sure he got it before each game. It was important to me to let him know just how much I was pulling for him and for the team. I figured any little motivation when it was getting hard might help him through the game. On a couple of occasions Robbie put my message in his pads and played the entire game with it in there. By the time he got to college after the second game, we stopped the ritual. But for his last football game I did send him this note; I don't think he would mind me sharing it with you. It encapsulates everything that I've written about here.

Dear Robbie,

Is it possible today is your last college football game? I wanted to send you this note and tell you how so very proud I am of you. You are truly special in so many ways. You have grown into an exceptional young man both on and off the field. You have represented your school, your team, your family and yourself with honor, which gives us all reason to celebrate you today.

The only thing wrong with the game of football is when it is over, it is over. You never get to smell that sweaty helmet again or have the satisfaction of hearing the cheering crowd yell your name. Unlike other sports you can't get a pick-up game of full contact football going. Enjoy every second of today's game. This will also be the last time you play with these particular set of guys you are so close too. I watched you the last couple of years take the younger players under your wing and help them. You have grown into a real leader and have inspired more people than you could ever realize.

I have watched you play since you were six years old and have loved every single second of the experience. Thank you for sharing it so closely with me. On Saturday when the final whistle blows I'm not sure what I will be doing on the outside, but know that on the inside I will be crying.

Tears come in all forms, but mostly from sadness or happiness. If by chance you do catch me tearing up it will be because of an overwhelming sense of pride I have for you.

You go out Saturday have fun and celebrate all the glory that is yours. Then, it's on to your fifth quarter. And in the fifth quarter I will still be your biggest supporter, cheering you on all the way.

Nothing but love
Dad

During Robbie's games in college, I could never sit still. I'd catch myself twisting my body in the stands to help Robbie break a tackle or fake out a defensive play. In my mind I felt the pain from a big hit, the excitement from a win or a big play, and the disappointment from a loss or a miscue. I once had to explain to someone sitting next to me that I was not being unsocial during a game because I wasn't talking to them. In my mind, when I watched Robbie play, there was just the two of us. I watched him on the sidelines and on the field as if I could read his mind, feeling what he was feeling or thinking what he was thinking, reading his mood and body language.

I think I learned how to do that from my mother. When I was playing Pop Warner football, my mother used to dress me in bright red socks. She said she did that so she could always tell me apart from all the other kids. When I played in high school football, she would be waiting for me when I got home regardless of how late it was so she could relive every play of the game with me. Finally I asked her how she was so in tune with every thing I did on field. That's when she told me she never really watched the game; she just watched everything I did. So that's exactly how I enjoyed watching all of my son's games.

Some of the Rice fans used to tease me a bit during Robbie's freshmen year. I was the dad who never sat still in the stands. When he was younger, I was one of his coaches so I was used to being on the side lines walking up and down the field getting as close to the action as possible. When he was in high school and they needed someone to work the chains, I couldn't wait to volunteer. This allowed me to again get the best vantage point and to walk up and down the field. In college I had to sit in the stands and contain myself, kind of. It was typical for me to sit in ten different places during one of Robbie's games. His first game in college, I walked up and down the stadium stairs more than twenty times trying to get the best view of the action. I didn't even realize I was doing this until the other parents started teasing me about where I was going to sit at the next game.

I got such a thrill when Robbie made a good play and everyone turned to congratulate me, as if I made the play. But my real thrill came from knowing that every time Robbie succeeded in the field, he was creating a positive memory that would last him a life time and help him in his fifth quarter. Robbie never missed a game due to an injury, from the time he was six years old to his last game at twenty-two. He certainly was not going to miss his first opportunity to start on the varsity. On about the third offensive series Robbie took the ball eighty yards for his first of many touchdowns. As Robbie was celebrating in the end zone, a few people turned to me to say congratulations and asked me how it felt. I recall this like it was yesterday. I felt so stupid because I was so choked up and working hard to fight back my tears, so the only way I could respond was to shake my head.

I miss the butterflies I got during close games. I miss being the Sunday morning coach or running downstairs to the lobby of the hotel to get the paper to see what they said about Rob and to search for his picture. It's thrilling to watch your son sign autographs or give a television interview.

Robbie was always articulate and was very good in those interviews, passing most of the credit he might be receiving onto his coaches and teammates. I also miss those moments I got to watch how gentle and caring he was to all the little kids who would ask him for his wristbands or for an autograph after a hard fought win or loss. Yes, I will miss every bit of the football experience we shared. But I'm more excited about his fifth quarter.

Robbie Beck might not be a Bronco, a Silver Bullet, a War Eagle, or a Fighting Owl any longer. He is and always had been much more than a football player; he is my son whom I love and cherish more than I could ever express in words. Robbie and I always have had a very special bond. Football only enhanced it. Helping him, teaching him, supporting him through his football career gave me a platform to teach him many life lessons that he can use for the rest of his life.

I have a different and special bond with each one of my four children. Today, I look forward to helping, teaching, and supporting them in their new ventures and endeavors, too. I relish the opportunity to see their excitement and fulfillment as they use the principal secrets of football to succeed in their fifth quarter.

I feel the same hope and excitement for you, and for your success in the fifth quarter. You might not have been a star college athlete like Robbie Beck or a pro ball player earning a seven figure income or even a high school player. Yes, because you have read this book, regardless of your past, you are now prepared as well as anyone who ever played the game of football to go out and make your mark.

At some point, all football players play their last game. Maybe it's their senior year in high school or college; maybe it's after a long, successful professional football career, *but the game does end.* However,_there is no ending season, or final game in the game of life. The game goes on every hour of every day.

It's the game of life and it's the one that really counts. And if you played football, know that while there are no more cheering crowds, newspapers or TV interviews in this game, no more supportive coaches helping you with every step, it doesn't mean that you are alone. All those coaches and all those other supporters who helped you accomplish the courage to even put on a helmet and walk out on the field or set school records will remain as passengers on your bus. However, this bus isn't simply taking you to the next football game; instead, it's the mental bus of life packed full of helpful lessons, memories and experiences. This bus is going down the road of life with the destination—success! There will be opponents and obstacles to overcome just like in the game of football. With the same kind of practice, preparation, as well as continuing to apply the principles discussed throughout this book, any player is in the drivers' seat of their own bus.

If you haven't played football, it doesn't matter. You have people who are cheering and supporting you through life as well, and the principle attributes of success are the same. You have your fifth quarter to play. Whether you are just beginning your fifth quarter or you are well into it, it's not too late to apply the principle secrets of football.

Football coaches at all levels, stress to their players, the fourth quarter is the most important quarter in football. The truth is, the *only* quarter that matters in the most important game anyone will play is in one's life—the fifth quarter. You know the secret of football. Success in the fifth quarter can be yours.

***

To Your Beginning—To Your 5th Quarter!

About the Author

BOB BECK IS AN AUTHOR, speaker, trainer and international business consultant.

In his youth, he was an accomplished athlete in many sports. Captain of his high school football team, he ranked number one in Ohio in solo tackles his senior year and went on to play college ball at Defiance College. He was a competitive swimmer for fourteen years and has also participated in water polo, basketball, baseball, soccer, wrestling, golf, and tennis.

Since he stopped playing competitive sports, Bob has been a highly successful entrepreneur. He has been an executive in three self-funded startups and led them through to public IPOs. Though he's a board member and executive partner with several firms, his primary business is

Sales Builders, Inc., of which he is founder and CEO. Sales Builders is a dedicated professional development firm, which offers training, consulting and revolutionary software to sales people on the front lines. He is also founded Bob Beck International, a company that holds workshops dedicated to helping individuals become more successful and fulfilled.

Bob developed the popular "Quid Pro Quo" series of sales training courses, which are now being taught nationwide, and in seven foreign countries. Bob's "Trusted Advisor" bloglet is ranked number nineteen out of more than 10,000 for most visited and informative.

In 1999, Bob was invited to contribute to *Inc.* Magazine's book, *310 Great Ideas for Selling Smarter.* He is the author of *Mutual Respect* (90 Minute Books, 2005), has published articles in a number of business magazines, and has written several white papers on the topic of successful selling.

But Bob's first love is connecting directly with people about how to succeed in today's competitive business environments. A popular, in-demand speaker at sales and marketing conferences, he travels the world sharing the experiences, stories, and viewpoints that provide the framework for *Winning in the 5th Quarter.*

Bonus!!

OFTENTIMES I FIND THAT motivational or self-help books get their readers all excited and fired up, but they don't leave the reader with anything to *do* with all that fire.

If you like what you read here in *Winning in the 5ᵗʰ Quarter*, you'll love what my *free* gift will do for your own fifth quarter in life!

I sincerely want to help, so I'm offering you my *Winning in the 5ᵗʰ Quarter: Your Playbook for Life* for **free**! It is designed to follow the path I outline in the book. You get your pre-season workout and a pre-game planning program. You'll find a wealth of targeted exercises to take you through the four quarters of your game so that you can live life successfully in *your* fifth quarter!!

Go to www.BobBeckInternational.com, and click on the button that says "Score." Download your *free* copy of the *Winning in the 5ᵗʰ Quarter: Your Playbook for Life* right away! It's in a pdf format, so all you have to do is print it off and you can start applying the secrets of football to your life immediately!

And, as an additional bonus, when you visit www.BobBeckinternational.com, you will find thousands of dollars in additional giveaways all designed to help you.

Visit me on the web today and see the results of true success in action. Don't even think about waiting. Acting is one of your success principles—do it now!

To your 5th quarter!

Bob Beck

P.S. And, just to sweeten the pot, I will come speak to your group or for your event for 15 percent off my normal direct-speaking fee. Trust me, that is worth far more than the cost of the book! Mention the number 41 when you call to inquire.

Printed in the United States
205977BV00002B/1-102/P